Saree Saga: Unveiling the Enchanting World of Six Yards

In a tapestry of timeless elegance, cultural heritage, and artistic finesse, the saree stands as a symbol of grace and sophistication. Woven with threads of tradition and draped with stories of generations past, the saree encapsulates the essence of the diverse and vibrant cultures of India. Its intricate weaves, vivid colors, and exquisite designs have captivated the hearts of people across the globe.

Welcome to "Saree Saga: Unveiling the Enchanting World of Six Yards," a journey that celebrates the rich heritage and allure of this iconic garment. Through the pages of this book, we embark on a captivating exploration of the saree's history, craftsmanship, regional variations, and the profound significance it holds in the lives of millions.

From the bustling lanes of Varanasi, where artisans meticulously handcraft intricate Banarasi sarees, to the ethereal beauty of Kanjeevaram sarees that tell stories of ancient Tamil traditions, we delve into the diverse universe of sarees. We unravel the secrets of the lush silk sarees of Kanchipuram, the delicate artistry of Chanderi sarees, and the vibrant hues of Bandhani sarees that embody the spirit of Rajasthan. Each chapter unfurls a new chapter in the narrative of sarees, exploring the distinct weaving techniques, motifs, and cultural influences that make each region's saree a masterpiece in its own right.

But "Saree Saga" is more than a chronicle of fabric and design; it is a celebration of the women who don this six-yard wonder. Weaving together stories of women from all walks of life, we delve into the emotional and personal connections they have with the saree. From grandmothers passing down their treasured sarees to the younger generation to empowered women redefining saree draping styles, we witness the saree's power to evoke memories, preserve traditions, and shape identities.

This book is an invitation to embrace the enchanting world of sarees—a world where heritage meets contemporary fashion, where artistic brilliance intertwines with cultural narratives, and where every drape becomes a canvas for self-expression. It is a testament to the enduring legacy of the saree, which continues to evolve and inspire new generations.

Join us on this captivating journey through "Saree Saga: Unveiling the Enchanting World of Six Yards" as we pay homage to the elegance, craftsmanship, and timeless beauty of the saree, an emblem of grace and tradition that transcends borders and captivates hearts.

I. Introduction

- Definition and significance of sarees
- Historical background and cultural significance
- Evolution of saree fashion and trends

II. Types of Sarees

- Traditional sarees:
  - Kanjivaram sarees
  - Banarasi sarees
  - Chanderi sarees
  - Paithani sarees
  - Bandhani sarees

- Regional sarees:
  - Bengal tant sarees
  - Odisha ikat sarees
  - Gujarati patola sarees
  - South Indian silk sarees
  - Maharashtrian nauvari sarees

III. Saree Draping Styles

- Nivi style (commonly worn in North India)
- Bengali style (distinctive draping style of Bengal)
- Maharashtrian style (nauvari saree draping)
- Tamilian style (Madisar and Pudavai draping)
- Gujarati style (seedha pallu and front pallu draping)

IV. Sarees in Different Occasions

- Bridal sarees and wedding ensembles
- Festive sarees
- Office and formal wear sarees
- Casual and daily wear sarees
- Special occasion sarees (parties, receptions, etc.)

V. Saree Fabrics and Embellishments

- Silk sarees
- Cotton sarees
- Georgette, chiffon, and crepe sarees
- Embroidery, zari work, and embellishments
- Saree borders and motifs

VI. Saree Styling and Accessories

- Blouse designs and trends
- Saree jewelry and accessories
- Hairstyles and makeup to complement sarees

Definition and significance of sarees

Sarees are traditional Indian garments that hold deep cultural significance and are cherished for their beauty, elegance, and versatility. A saree is a long piece of fabric, typically measuring six yards in length, that is draped around the body in various styles to create a graceful and flattering silhouette.

Significance of Sarees:

1. Cultural Heritage: Sarees are a reflection of India's rich cultural heritage and diverse regional traditions. Each state and community in India has its unique weaving techniques, patterns, and motifs that are passed down through generations, preserving the cultural identity and artistic legacy of the region.

2. Symbol of Femininity: Sarees have been an integral part of Indian women's attire for centuries, symbolizing femininity, grace, and elegance. The way a woman drapes her saree reflects her personal style and individuality.

3. Versatility: Sarees offer immense versatility, allowing women to adapt their draping style to various occasions, from formal events to everyday wear. The same saree can be draped in different ways, allowing for creative interpretations and expressing one's personal flair.

4. Artistry and Craftsmanship: Sarees are a testament to the exquisite craftsmanship and intricate artistry of Indian weavers. From handloom sarees created by skilled artisans to embellished silk sarees adorned with intricate embroidery or hand-painted designs, each saree is a work of art.

5. Bridging Generations: Sarees hold sentimental value as heirlooms that are passed down from one generation to another. They carry the memories and stories of ancestors, connecting present-day wearers to their cultural roots and family history.

6. Occasions and Celebrations: Sarees are often worn during special occasions and celebrations, such as weddings, festivals, and religious ceremonies. They embody the spirit of celebration, adding a touch of elegance and grandeur to these significant events.

7. Global Appeal: In recent years, sarees have gained international recognition and have become a fashion statement worldwide. Fashion enthusiasts and designers from around the globe have embraced the beauty and craftsmanship of sarees, incorporating them into contemporary designs and showcasing them on global platforms.

The significance of sarees goes beyond being just a garment; they represent the cultural fabric of India and serve as a source of pride, beauty, and timeless elegance.

Historical background and cultural significance

The history of sarees can be traced back thousands of years, making them one of the oldest known garments in the world. The exact origins of sarees are uncertain, as they have evolved over time through various influences and cultural exchanges.

Ancient texts and sculptures from as early as the Indus Valley Civilization depict women draped in garments similar to sarees. Over the centuries, sarees underwent transformations influenced by different dynasties, regional customs, and foreign invasions. The art of weaving and embellishing sarees flourished in different parts of India, each region developing its distinctive style and technique.

Cultural Significance:

Sarees hold immense cultural significance in India and are deeply ingrained in the traditions, rituals, and everyday life of Indian women. They serve as a symbol of identity, femininity, and cultural heritage. Here are some aspects of their cultural significance:

1. Regional Diversity: India's diverse culture is reflected in the numerous styles of sarees, each associated with a specific region or community. From the vibrant and intricately woven Banarasi sarees of Varanasi to the colorful and geometric patterns of Bandhani sarees from Gujarat, sarees showcase the unique artistry and traditions of different regions.

2. Festivals and Celebrations: Sarees are an integral part of festivals and celebratory occasions in India. Women adorn themselves with exquisite sarees during religious festivals like Diwali, Durga Puja, and Navratri, as well as during weddings and other significant ceremonies. Sarees play a crucial role in enhancing the festive spirit and creating a sense of elegance and grandeur.

3. Bridal Attire: Sarees hold a special place in Indian weddings, where they are often the preferred choice for the bride. Bridal sarees are richly embellished with intricate embroidery, zari work, and precious stones, symbolizing opulence and the bride's auspicious journey into married life.

4. Social Significance: Sarees are often worn on formal and social occasions, such as family gatherings, religious functions, and cultural events. They are seen as a mark of respect and adherence to traditional values, showcasing a woman's grace and dignity.

5. Handloom Heritage: Handloom sarees, woven by skilled artisans using traditional techniques, are cherished for their craftsmanship and cultural significance. These sarees promote sustainable livelihoods for weavers and contribute to the preservation of traditional weaving practices and heritage.

6. Revival of Artistic Traditions: Sarees have played a pivotal role in reviving and sustaining traditional textile arts and crafts. By supporting handloom sarees and artisans, wearers contribute to the preservation of these art forms, empowering weavers and promoting sustainable fashion.

Sarees represent more than just a garment; they embody the rich tapestry of Indian culture, heritage, and craftsmanship. They serve as a medium to express artistic creativity, celebrate traditions, and foster a sense of community and pride among wearers. With their timeless beauty and cultural significance, sarees continue to captivate hearts and minds, transcending boundaries and generations.

Evolution of saree fashion and trends

Saree fashion has evolved significantly over the years, reflecting changing tastes, societal influences, and global trends. While the essence of a saree remains the same—a six-yard drape—the styles, patterns, fabrics, and draping techniques have witnessed remarkable transformations. Here is a glimpse into the evolution of saree fashion and trends:

1. Traditional Weaves and Styles: The traditional saree weaves like Banarasi, Kanjeevaram, and Chanderi have stood the test of time and continue to be highly sought after. These sarees are known for their intricate motifs, rich silk fabrics, and exquisite craftsmanship. Traditional saree styles such as Nauvari (Maharashtrian), Paithani (Maharashtrian), and Pochampally (Telugu) have also maintained their popularity and cultural significance.

2. Contemporary Fusion: With the influence of global fashion trends, contemporary fusion sarees have gained popularity. These sarees blend traditional techniques with modern designs, creating a unique fusion of styles. Fusion sarees may incorporate elements like unconventional fabrics, experimental drapes, and contemporary motifs, catering to the tastes of the modern woman.

3. Designer Sarees: The emergence of designer sarees has revolutionized the saree industry. Renowned fashion designers have introduced innovative concepts, experimenting with fabrics, patterns, and embellishments. Designer sarees showcase a blend of

traditional craftsmanship and contemporary aesthetics, appealing to fashion-forward individuals who seek unique and high-end creations.

4. Revival of Handloom: In recent years, there has been a renewed appreciation for handloom sarees. Weavers and artisans have been celebrated for their skill and dedication to preserving traditional techniques. Handloom sarees, characterized by their intricate weaves and rich heritage, have witnessed a revival, creating a sustainable and socially conscious fashion movement.

5. Contemporary Draping Styles: Draping styles have evolved to reflect modern preferences and lifestyles. While the classic Nivi drape remains popular, newer draping techniques have gained popularity, such as the butterfly drape, the lehenga-style drape, and the pant-style drape. These innovative draping styles add a contemporary twist to the traditional saree, offering versatility and ease of wear.

6. Experimentation with Fabrics and Colors: Saree designers have been experimenting with fabrics and colors to offer a diverse range of options. Alongside traditional silk and cotton sarees, lighter fabrics like georgette, chiffon, and crepe have gained prominence for their fluidity and comfort. Additionally, contemporary sarees often feature bold and vibrant colors, as well as unique combinations and contrasts.

7. Embellishments and Embroidery: Embellishments and embroidery play a significant role in saree fashion. Traditional techniques like zari work, thread work, and mirror work continue to be popular. However, contemporary sarees have also embraced modern embellishments, such as sequins, beads, and unconventional materials, adding a touch of glamour and sparkle.

The evolution of saree fashion and trends showcases the adaptability of this traditional garment to changing times. From classic weaves that have stood the test of time to contemporary fusion styles that embrace global influences, sarees continue to captivate the fashion world. Whether it's a traditional handloom saree or a designer creation, sarees offer a timeless elegance that celebrates the beauty and diversity of Indian fashion.

Kanjivaram sarees

Kanjivaram sarees, also known as Kanchipuram sarees, are renowned for their exquisite craftsmanship, rich silk fabric, and intricate designs. Originating from the town of Kanchipuram in Tamil Nadu, India, these sarees have a long-standing legacy that dates back several centuries. Kanjivaram sarees are treasured for their opulence, durability, and traditional appeal, making them an integral part of Indian weddings, festivals, and special occasions.

1. Silk and Zari: Kanjivaram sarees are crafted from pure mulberry silk, which is known for its lustrous texture and durability. The silk threads used in these sarees are sourced from South India, ensuring their authenticity and quality. One of the distinguishing features of Kanjivaram sarees is the intricate zari work, which involves weaving fine gold or silver threads into the fabric. The zari work often features motifs inspired by temples, nature, mythology, and traditional designs.

2. Traditional Weaving Techniques: Kanjivaram sarees are woven using traditional handloom techniques that have been passed down through generations of skilled weavers. These weavers, often from the Sankarankovil region, meticulously create the sarees on handlooms, employing techniques that require exceptional precision and artistry. The weaving process involves combining multiple silk threads to create a strong and durable fabric, resulting in sarees that can last for generations.

3. Intricate Designs and Motifs: Kanjivaram sarees are known for their intricate and elaborate designs. The

borders of the sarees are adorned with intricately woven patterns, including traditional motifs like peacocks, flowers, checks, paisleys, and temple designs. The pallu, the loose end of the saree, is often the highlight of the Kanjivaram saree, featuring grand designs and rich zari work. The interplay of colors and motifs in these sarees creates a visually stunning and captivating effect.

4. Vibrant Colors and Combinations: Kanjivaram sarees are available in a wide range of vibrant colors, ranging from traditional shades like red, maroon, and gold to contemporary hues like pastels and jewel tones. The color combinations in Kanjivaram sarees are carefully chosen to enhance the beauty of the designs and create a harmonious blend of shades.

5. Symbol of Elegance and Tradition: Kanjivaram sarees are considered a symbol of elegance, grace, and tradition. They are highly valued for their timeless appeal and are often passed down as heirlooms within families. Kanjivaram sarees are sought after by brides for their bridal trousseau and are worn with pride during weddings and festive occasions.

6. Global Recognition: Kanjivaram sarees have gained global recognition for their exquisite craftsmanship and cultural significance. They have been showcased on international runways, worn by celebrities, and appreciated by fashion enthusiasts around the world. The artistry and intricacy of Kanjivaram sarees continue to captivate and inspire designers, fashion connoisseurs, and saree lovers worldwide.

Kanjivaram sarees are a testament to the rich cultural heritage and craftsmanship of India. They exemplify the beauty of traditional weaving techniques and represent the cultural diversity and artistic excellence of Tamil Nadu. Whether it's the intricate zari work, the vibrant colors, or the timeless designs, Kanjivaram sarees hold a special place in the hearts of saree enthusiasts, symbolizing the timeless elegance and regal charm of Indian ethnic wear.

enthusiasts, symbolizing the timeless elegance and regal charm of Indian ethnic wear.

Banarasi sarees

Banarasi sarees are one of the most revered and cherished forms of traditional Indian sarees. Originating from the holy city of Varanasi (formerly known as Banaras) in Uttar Pradesh, India, these sarees are renowned for their opulent silk fabric, intricate designs, and timeless beauty. With a history that spans several centuries, Banarasi sarees have become an epitome of elegance and grandeur, captivating women across generations.

1. Silk and Zari Work: Banarasi sarees are predominantly crafted from pure silk, which is known for its luxurious texture and sheen. The silk used in Banarasi sarees is of the highest quality, sourced from different parts of India. What sets Banarasi sarees apart is the exquisite zari work, which involves the use of metallic threads, usually gold or silver, woven into the fabric. The zari work is meticulously done by skilled artisans, creating intricate patterns and motifs that add a touch of glamour and richness to the saree.

2. Intricate Weaving Techniques: The making of Banarasi sarees involves intricate weaving techniques, primarily done on handlooms. The weaving process is time-consuming and requires the expertise of skilled craftsmen who have honed their artistry over generations. The sarees are woven with precision using various loom types, such as Jacquard and Pitlooms, to create intricate patterns and designs. The weaving techniques used in Banarasi sarees are traditional and have been passed down through generations, preserving the authenticity and craftsmanship of these sarees.

3. Motifs and Designs: Banarasi sarees are known for their elaborate motifs and designs that reflect a blend of Indian cultural heritage and Mughal influences. The most common motifs found in Banarasi sarees include floral patterns, leaves, paisleys, butis (small motifs), and intricate brocade work. The designs are often inspired by nature, mythology, and architectural elements, creating a tapestry of visual beauty and artistic expression. The borders and pallu (loose end) of the saree are adorned with elaborate designs and zari work, adding to the grandeur and elegance of the saree.

4. Varied Styles and Types: Banarasi sarees come in various styles and types, each showcasing unique characteristics and weaving techniques. Some popular types of Banarasi sarees include the pure silk Katan sarees, the heavy brocade Jamawar sarees, the lightweight Organza sarees, and the georgette-based Banarasi sarees. Each type has its own distinct appeal, catering to different preferences and occasions.

5. Bridal and Festive Wear: Banarasi sarees are highly sought after for bridal wear and are considered a symbol of grandeur and tradition. These sarees are often adorned with intricate designs, heavy zari work, and vibrant colors, making them a perfect choice for weddings and special occasions. Banarasi sarees are also favored during festivals, cultural events, and celebratory gatherings, where they add a touch of regality and grace to the wearer.

6. Heritage and Cultural Significance: Banarasi sarees hold immense cultural significance and are considered a valuable part of India's heritage. They are deeply rooted in Indian traditions and are associated with auspicious occasions and rituals. The art of weaving Banarasi sarees has been passed down through generations, with weavers dedicating their lives to preserving this traditional craft. The making of Banarasi sarees involves

a close-knit community of weavers, artisans, and craftsmen, who contribute their skills and knowledge to create these exquisite pieces of art.

Banarasi sarees have not only captivated the hearts of Indian women but have also gained international acclaim for their beauty and craftsmanship. They have graced runways, adorned celebrities, and become a symbol of Indian elegance and craftsmanship on a global scale. The allure and charm of Banarasi sarees continue to endure, transcending time and trends, as they remain a timeless embodiment of the rich cultural heritage and artistic excellence of India.

Chanderi sarees

Chanderi sarees are renowned for their sheer elegance, delicate texture, and exquisite craftsmanship. Originating from the town of Chanderi in Madhya Pradesh, India, these sarees hold a special place in the hearts of saree connoisseurs and enthusiasts. Known for their fine handwoven fabric and intricate embellishments, Chanderi sarees embody the essence of grace and sophistication.

1. Chanderi Fabric: The hallmark of Chanderi sarees is the fabric itself, which is lightweight, sheer, and breathable. The fabric is traditionally woven using a combination of silk and cotton threads, resulting in a luxurious texture and a subtle shimmer. The unique blend of these fibers gives Chanderi sarees their distinct drape and comfort, making them ideal for both formal occasions and everyday wear.

2. Weaving Techniques: Chanderi sarees are meticulously woven on handlooms, employing traditional weaving techniques that have been passed down through generations. The weaving process involves the use of fine silk or cotton threads, which are carefully interlaced to create intricate patterns and motifs. One of the distinguishing features of Chanderi sarees is the transparent or sheer sections, known as "Khaddi," which add a touch of ethereal beauty to the fabric.

3. Designs and Motifs: Chanderi sarees feature a wide array of designs and motifs, ranging from traditional to contemporary. The most popular motifs include butis (small motifs), floral patterns, peacocks, geometric shapes, and delicate hand-painted designs. These motifs

are often rendered using zari (metallic thread), resham (silk thread), or hand-block printing techniques, adding an artistic and vibrant appeal to the saree.

4. Embellishments: Chanderi sarees are known for their intricate embellishments that enhance their beauty and allure. The sarees are adorned with exquisite embroidery, zari work, sequins, and beadwork, adding a touch of opulence and glamour. The embellishments are meticulously crafted by skilled artisans, who bring life to the fabric through their intricate detailing and craftsmanship.

5. Versatility and Occasions: Chanderi sarees are versatile and can be worn for a variety of occasions, ranging from formal events to casual gatherings. They are favored as bridal wear, festive attire, and even for corporate settings. Chanderi sarees strike the perfect balance between elegance and comfort, making them a popular choice among women of all ages.

6. Cultural Heritage: Chanderi sarees are deeply rooted in the cultural heritage of India. The weaving of Chanderi fabric and the creation of Chanderi sarees have been traditional crafts passed down through generations. The artistry and skill involved in the making of Chanderi sarees have earned recognition and protection as Geographical Indication (GI) tags, ensuring the authenticity and quality of these timeless garments.

Chanderi sarees encapsulate the essence of tradition, artistry, and timeless elegance. They are a celebration of Indian craftsmanship and a testament to the creativity and skill of the weavers. Adorning a Chanderi saree is not just wearing a garment but experiencing the beauty and legacy of a rich cultural heritage.

Paithani sarees

Paithani sarees, named after the town of Paithan in Maharashtra, India, are renowned for their opulence, rich heritage, and intricate craftsmanship. These sarees are considered to be a symbol of tradition and elegance, cherished by women across generations. With their vibrant colors, exquisite silk fabric, and intricate motifs, Paithani sarees are a testament to the artistry and skill of the weavers.

1. Silk and Zari Weaving: Paithani sarees are traditionally woven using pure silk threads, giving them a lustrous and luxurious appearance. The weaving technique involves the use of zari, which is a metallic thread made of fine gold or silver-coated copper. The zari is intricately woven into the fabric, creating beautiful patterns and motifs that shimmer and catch the light.

2. Traditional Motifs: Paithani sarees are known for their elaborate motifs inspired by nature, such as peacocks, flowers, vines, and geometrical designs. These motifs are woven into the fabric using the tapestry technique, where each thread is individually hand-woven to create the intricate patterns. The motifs often have symbolic meanings and reflect the cultural heritage of Maharashtra.

3. Pallu and Borders: One of the distinguishing features of Paithani sarees is their ornate pallu (the decorative end piece of the saree) and borders. The pallu is usually adorned with intricate designs, including peacocks, lotus flowers, and other traditional motifs. The borders are also intricately woven and can feature geometric

patterns or intricate floral designs.

4. Colorful Palette: Paithani sarees are known for their vibrant and striking colors. Traditional Paithani sarees often feature a combination of contrasting colors, such as red and green, purple and gold, or blue and yellow. These vibrant color combinations add to the visual appeal of the saree and make them a perfect choice for special occasions and festivals.

5. Traditional Craftsmanship: The art of Paithani weaving has been passed down through generations, with skilled artisans dedicating their expertise to create these exquisite sarees. The weaving process requires precision, patience, and attention to detail. Each Paithani saree is a labor of love and takes several weeks or even months to complete, showcasing the meticulous craftsmanship involved.

6. Cultural Heritage: Paithani sarees hold immense cultural significance in Maharashtra and are considered a treasured part of its heritage. They are often worn on special occasions such as weddings, festivals, and religious ceremonies. Paithani sarees have also been granted Geographical Indication (GI) status, recognizing their uniqueness and protecting their authenticity.

Paithani sarees are not just garments; they are a symbol of tradition, craftsmanship, and timeless beauty. They embody the rich cultural heritage of Maharashtra and have transcended time to remain an integral part of Indian ethnic wear. Adorning a Paithani saree is not only a fashion statement but also a tribute to the exquisite artistry and legacy of the weavers who have preserved this art form for generations.

Bandhani sarees

Bandhani sarees, also known as Bandhej or Bandhni sarees, are a traditional form of tie-dye art that originates from the western states of India, particularly Gujarat and Rajasthan. These sarees are known for their vibrant colors, intricate patterns, and the unique technique used to create them. Bandhani sarees have a rich cultural heritage and hold a special place in Indian ethnic fashion.

1. Tie-Dye Art: Bandhani is a tie-dye technique in which small portions of the fabric are tied tightly with threads, creating intricate patterns and designs. The tied fabric is then dyed in vibrant colors, and the tied portions resist the dye, resulting in a beautiful pattern when the threads are untied. The process requires skill and precision to achieve the desired design and color combinations.

2. Artisanal Craftsmanship: Bandhani sarees are handmade by skilled artisans who have mastered the art of tie-dye. The process involves tying thousands of small knots to create various patterns and motifs on the fabric. Each knot is tied by hand, making each saree unique and a work of art. The precision and expertise of the artisans contribute to the exquisite beauty of Bandhani sarees.

3. Patterns and Motifs: Bandhani sarees feature a wide range of patterns and motifs, including dots, squares, waves, and geometric shapes. These patterns are meticulously created using the tie-dye technique, resulting in intricate and visually stunning designs. Bandhani sarees often showcase traditional motifs such

as flowers, peacocks, elephants, and paisley, reflecting the cultural heritage and symbolism of the region.

4. Vibrant Colors: Bandhani sarees are known for their vibrant color palette. They are often dyed in bold and contrasting colors such as red, yellow, green, blue, and pink. The vibrant hues add a festive and celebratory vibe to the sarees, making them a popular choice for special occasions, weddings, and festivals.

5. Versatility and Appeal: Bandhani sarees are versatile and can be worn for both formal and casual occasions. The intricate patterns and vibrant colors make them eye-catching and elegant. Bandhani sarees are often paired with contrasting blouses and accessorized with traditional jewelry to complete the ethnic look. They are loved by women of all ages and have a timeless appeal that transcends fashion trends.

6. Cultural Significance: Bandhani sarees have deep cultural significance in Gujarat and Rajasthan. They are an integral part of the region's traditional attire and are often worn during weddings, festivals, and other auspicious occasions. Bandhani sarees are also considered auspicious and are believed to bring good luck and prosperity to the wearer.

Bandhani sarees represent the rich cultural heritage and craftsmanship of Gujarat and Rajasthan. They are a celebration of color, tradition, and artistry. Wearing a Bandhani saree is not just about donning a beautiful garment; it is embracing the centuries-old tie-dye technique and honoring the skilled artisans who have preserved this art form. Bandhani sarees are a testament to the beauty and diversity of Indian textiles and continue to captivate fashion enthusiasts with their timeless elegance.

Bengal tant sarees

Bengal Tant sarees, also known as Bengali cotton sarees, are a traditional handwoven textile art form that originates from the Indian state of West Bengal. These sarees are renowned for their lightweight and breathable cotton fabric, intricate weaving techniques, and elegant designs. Bengal Tant sarees hold a special place in the cultural heritage of Bengal and are considered an epitome of grace and tradition.

1. Fine Cotton Fabric: Bengal Tant sarees are crafted using fine and lightweight cotton yarns. The cotton used is known for its high-quality and comfort, making these sarees ideal for the warm and humid climate of Bengal. The soft and breathable fabric allows for ease of movement and drapes beautifully, adding to the wearer's comfort.

2. Handwoven Craftsmanship: Bengal Tant sarees are meticulously handwoven by skilled artisans, often belonging to weaving communities such as the Tanti community of Bengal. The sarees are woven on traditional handlooms, where the weaver manually interlaces the warp and weft threads to create the intricate patterns. The art of weaving Tant sarees has been passed down through generations, showcasing the expertise and craftsmanship of the weavers.

3. Jamdani Weaving Technique: One of the distinctive features of Bengal Tant sarees is the intricate Jamdani weaving technique. Jamdani involves adding supplementary weft threads to create motifs and patterns on the saree. These motifs can be floral,

geometric, or artistic designs. The Jamdani weaving technique requires skill and precision, and the weavers spend hours painstakingly weaving each motif into the fabric, resulting in breathtakingly beautiful designs.

4. Elegant Designs and Patterns: Bengal Tant sarees are known for their elegant and intricate designs. The sarees often feature delicate motifs inspired by nature, such as flowers, leaves, and vines. The patterns can be small and scattered or large and bold, depending on the design. The simplicity and sophistication of the designs make Bengal Tant sarees suitable for both formal and casual occasions.

5. Variety of Colors: Bengal Tant sarees are available in a wide range of colors, ranging from vibrant and bold shades to subtle and pastel hues. Traditional colors like red, white, and blue are commonly used, along with contemporary shades that cater to changing fashion trends. The color combinations are carefully chosen to enhance the beauty of the motifs and patterns woven into the saree.

6. Cultural Significance: Bengal Tant sarees have a significant cultural and historical importance in West Bengal. They are an integral part of Bengali weddings, festivals, and other traditional occasions. Bengal Tant sarees represent the cultural identity of the region and hold a special place in the hearts of Bengali women. They are often handed down through generations as heirlooms, symbolizing the bond between the past and the present.

Bengal Tant sarees are a timeless representation of Bengal's rich textile heritage. They embody the essence of traditional craftsmanship and showcase the skill and dedication of the weavers. Wearing a Bengal Tant saree is not just about adorning oneself in a beautiful garment; it is embracing the cultural legacy and celebrating the artistry of handwoven textiles. These sarees are a blend of elegance, comfort, and tradition, and continue to be cherished by women who appreciate the allure of Bengal's textile heritage.

Odisha ikat sarees

Odisha Ikat sarees, also known as Odisha handloom sarees or Odisha Bandha sarees, are a traditional handwoven textile art form that originates from the state of Odisha, India. These sarees are renowned for their vibrant colors, intricate ikat patterns, and rich cultural heritage. Odisha Ikat sarees are a testament to the skill and artistry of the weavers of Odisha and are cherished for their unique and captivating designs.

1. Ikat Weaving Technique: The distinguishing feature of Odisha Ikat sarees is the ikat weaving technique used to create intricate patterns on the fabric. Ikat is a resist dyeing technique where the yarns are dyed before they are woven. The weavers meticulously tie and dye the warp and weft threads to create the desired patterns. When woven together, these dyed threads form mesmerizing motifs and designs on the saree. The ikat technique requires precision and expertise, and the weavers' skill is reflected in the flawless execution of the patterns.

2. Vibrant Colors: Odisha Ikat sarees are known for their vibrant and eye-catching colors. The use of natural dyes adds to the richness and depth of the hues. Traditional colors like red, black, yellow, and blue are prominent in these sarees, symbolizing cultural significance and aesthetics. The colors are skillfully blended to create harmonious combinations that enhance the beauty of the patterns.

3. Intricate Motifs and Designs: Odisha Ikat sarees feature a wide array of motifs and designs, inspired by nature,

mythology, and local traditions. These motifs can include flowers, animals, geometric patterns, temple designs, and traditional symbols. Each motif has a unique significance and represents the cultural heritage of Odisha. The intricacy and precision of the designs make Odisha Ikat sarees a visual delight, capturing the essence of the region's artistry.

4. Handwoven Craftsmanship: Odisha Ikat sarees are meticulously handwoven by skilled artisans using traditional handlooms. The weaving process involves carefully aligning the dyed yarns to create the desired patterns. The weavers' expertise is crucial in ensuring that the patterns align perfectly, resulting in a flawless saree. The time and effort invested in weaving each saree make it a labor of love and a symbol of the weaver's dedication to their craft.

5. Cultural Significance: Odisha Ikat sarees hold immense cultural significance in the state of Odisha. They are an integral part of traditional Odia weddings, festivals, and special occasions. The sarees are often passed down through generations as cherished heirlooms, representing the cultural heritage and the pride of the Odia community. Wearing an Odisha Ikat saree is not just a fashion statement; it is a celebration of the rich traditions and craftsmanship of the region.

6. Versatility and Elegance: Odisha Ikat sarees are known for their versatility and timeless elegance. They can be worn for both formal and casual occasions, as well as cultural events and celebrations. The lightweight fabric and comfortable drape of these sarees make them suitable for all seasons. The vibrant colors and intricate designs make a bold fashion statement, capturing attention and exuding a sense of grace and sophistication.

Odisha Ikat sarees are a testament to the cultural richness and artistic legacy of Odisha. They showcase the remarkable skills of the weavers and their ability to translate age-old traditions into breathtaking textile masterpieces. Owning and wearing an Odisha Ikat saree is not only a personal adornment but also a way to preserve and promote the cultural heritage of Odisha. These sarees carry with them the stories, craftsmanship, and beauty of a region known for its artistic brilliance.

Gujarati patola sarees

Gujarati Patola sarees are a revered and exquisite form of handwoven silk sarees that originate from the state of Gujarat in India. These sarees are renowned for their vibrant colors, intricate geometric patterns, and impeccable craftsmanship. Patola sarees are considered a symbol of cultural heritage and are highly treasured for their rich history and artistry.

1. Double Ikat Weaving Technique: One of the distinguishing features of Gujarati Patola sarees is the use of the double ikat weaving technique. Double ikat involves the precise alignment and weaving of both the warp and weft threads, where each thread is dyed separately before weaving. This intricate process requires immense skill and precision, as the patterns and colors on both sides of the fabric must align perfectly. The double ikat technique contributes to the uniqueness and complexity of Patola sarees.

2. Vibrant Colors and Patterns: Gujarati Patola sarees are renowned for their vibrant and striking colors. These sarees feature a dazzling array of hues, including rich reds, vibrant greens, deep blues, and opulent yellows. The color combinations are carefully selected and meticulously woven to create mesmerizing geometric patterns such as flowers, elephants, parrots, and peacocks. The symmetrical designs and precise motifs reflect the meticulous attention to detail and aesthetic sensibility of the weavers.

3. Silk Fabric and Fine Craftsmanship: Patola sarees are predominantly made of pure silk, which adds

to their luxurious appeal. The fine silk threads are expertly woven to create a smooth and lustrous fabric that drapes gracefully. The weaving process requires immense skill, as each thread needs to be aligned perfectly to maintain the integrity of the pattern. The intricate designs and flawless execution showcase the craftsmanship and dedication of the weavers, making each Patola saree a true work of art.

4. Cultural and Ritual Significance: Gujarati Patola sarees hold significant cultural and ritual importance in Gujarat. These sarees are traditionally worn by women during auspicious occasions, weddings, and festivals. Patola sarees are considered a symbol of prosperity, good luck, and social status. They are often passed down through generations as heirlooms, signifying the legacy and traditions of the family. Wearing a Patola saree is not only a fashion statement but also a way to connect with the rich cultural heritage and traditions of Gujarat.

5. Time-Intensive Craftsmanship: Creating a Patola saree is a time-intensive process that requires immense skill and patience. From preparing the silk threads and dyeing them with natural colors to the precise weaving of the intricate patterns, the entire process can take several months to complete. Each saree is a labor of love and a testament to the dedication and artistry of the weavers.

6. Global Recognition: Gujarati Patola sarees have gained global recognition and admiration for their exquisite beauty and craftsmanship. They have found a place on international runways and in the wardrobes of fashion enthusiasts worldwide. The meticulous craftsmanship, vibrant colors, and timeless appeal of Patola sarees continue to captivate and inspire designers and connoisseurs of fashion.

Gujarati Patola sarees are a true embodiment of the rich textile heritage and artistic brilliance of Gujarat. They represent the cultural identity and traditions of the region, showcasing the expertise and creativity of the weavers. Each Patola saree tells a story of the meticulous craftsmanship, vibrant colors, and timeless elegance that have been cherished for generations. Owning a Patola saree is not just owning a piece of clothing; it is embracing a legacy of art, culture, and tradition.

South Indian silk sarees

South Indian silk sarees are renowned for their exquisite craftsmanship, opulent designs, and rich cultural heritage. They are a testament to the vibrant traditions and artistic excellence of South India. These sarees are crafted with meticulous care and attention to detail, making them highly coveted among saree enthusiasts across the world. Let's delve into the key aspects of South Indian silk sarees:

1. Pure Silk Fabric: South Indian silk sarees are primarily made from pure silk, known for its luxurious texture and lustrous sheen. The silk used in these sarees is sourced from silkworms, with the most common variety being mulberry silk. The fine silk threads are carefully woven to create a smooth and drapable fabric that exudes elegance.

2. Intricate Weaving Techniques: South Indian silk sarees are woven using various traditional techniques, such as Kanchipuram, Mysore, and Uppada. Each technique has its unique characteristics and motifs. For example, Kanchipuram silk sarees are renowned for their heavy silk fabric, intricate zari work, and temple-inspired designs. Mysore silk sarees are known for their lightweight and breathable fabric, adorned with delicate embellishments. Uppada silk sarees showcase a distinctive jamdani weaving technique, where the patterns are created by interweaving additional silk threads.

3. Rich Colors and Designs: South Indian silk sarees are characterized by their vibrant colors and elaborate

designs. They feature a wide range of hues, from deep and bold shades to pastel and muted tones. The designs on these sarees often incorporate traditional motifs like peacocks, flowers, paisleys, and religious symbols. The intricate zari work, which involves weaving metallic threads of gold or silver into the fabric, adds a touch of grandeur and richness to the sarees.

4. Cultural Significance: South Indian silk sarees hold immense cultural significance in the region. They are an integral part of weddings, festivals, and other auspicious occasions. In South Indian culture, silk sarees symbolize grace, beauty, and prosperity. They are considered heirlooms and are often passed down through generations as cherished family treasures. Wearing a South Indian silk saree is not just a fashion choice; it is a celebration of tradition, heritage, and cultural identity.

5. Skilled Artisans: The creation of South Indian silk sarees involves the expertise and craftsmanship of skilled artisans. These weavers, often from generations of traditional weaving families, possess exceptional skills and knowledge passed down through the ages. They meticulously weave each saree by hand, paying attention to every detail, ensuring the quality and beauty of the final product. The dedication and talent of these artisans are reflected in the exquisite South Indian silk sarees they produce.

6. Global Recognition: South Indian silk sarees have gained international acclaim for their timeless beauty and craftsmanship. They have graced international runways and are admired by fashion enthusiasts worldwide. The unique blend of traditional techniques, intricate designs, and luxurious silk fabric has captivated the attention of designers and connoisseurs of fashion.

South Indian silk sarees are not just garments; they are a reflection of the rich cultural heritage, skilled craftsmanship, and timeless elegance of South India. Owning a South Indian silk saree is embracing a piece of art that embodies tradition, craftsmanship, and beauty. These sarees continue to be cherished and adored by women who appreciate the splendor and grace they bring when draped.

Maharashtrian nauvari sarees

Maharashtrian Nauvari sarees, also known as Nauvari or Lugade sarees, are traditional garments worn by women in Maharashtra, a state in Western India. Nauvari literally translates to "nine-yard," referring to the length of the saree. These sarees hold a special place in Maharashtrian culture and are an epitome of tradition and grace. Let's explore the key aspects of Maharashtrian Nauvari sarees:

1. Unique Draping Style: The distinguishing feature of a Nauvari saree is its unique draping style. Unlike the regular saree draping, which involves wrapping the saree around the waist and pleating it at the front, the Nauvari saree is draped in a way that resembles a dhoti. The saree is tucked at the back, brought forward between the legs, and then draped over the shoulder, forming a beautiful pleated front. This draping style allows for greater mobility and ease of movement.

2. Traditional Maharashtrian Motifs: Maharashtrian Nauvari sarees often feature traditional motifs and designs that hold cultural significance. Common motifs include peacocks, lotuses, paisleys, and geometric patterns. These motifs are intricately woven or printed onto the saree, adding a touch of beauty and symbolism to the garment.

3. Vibrant Colors: Maharashtrian Nauvari sarees are known for their vibrant and lively colors. Traditionally, red, green, and yellow are the predominant colors seen in these sarees, reflecting the cultural heritage and festive spirit of Maharashtra. However, contemporary

designs now feature a wide range of colors, allowing women to express their personal style while maintaining the essence of the Nauvari saree.

4. Cultural Significance: Maharashtrian Nauvari sarees hold immense cultural significance and are deeply rooted in Maharashtrian traditions. They are commonly worn during festivals, weddings, and other auspicious occasions, symbolizing grace, elegance, and cultural identity. Nauvari sarees are also considered a symbol of women's empowerment and strength, reflecting the historical significance of Maratha warrior women who wore these sarees while participating in battles.

5. Versatile and Comfortable: Nauvari sarees are highly versatile and suitable for various occasions. They can be draped in different styles, allowing women to experiment with their look and create unique variations. The dhoti-style draping provides greater freedom of movement, making the Nauvari saree comfortable and practical for day-to-day activities, dance performances, and cultural events.

6. Preservation of Tradition: Maharashtrian Nauvari sarees have stood the test of time and continue to be embraced by women who value tradition and cultural heritage. The art of weaving Nauvari sarees is passed down through generations, preserving the craftsmanship and skills of traditional weavers. By wearing a Nauvari saree, women not only connect with their roots but also contribute to the preservation of a rich cultural legacy.

Maharashtrian Nauvari sarees are not just garments; they are a symbol of Maharashtrian culture, pride, and tradition. Wearing a Nauvari saree is an expression of identity, grace, and reverence for the vibrant heritage of Maharashtra. It is an ode to the rich craftsmanship and artistry of the weavers who bring these sarees to life.

Nivi style (commonly worn in North India)

The Nivi style is one of the most popular and commonly worn saree draping styles in North India, particularly in states like Punjab, Haryana, Uttar Pradesh, and Rajasthan. It is a graceful and elegant way of draping a saree that highlights the beauty of the garment and enhances the wearer's femininity. Let's explore the key features and steps involved in the Nivi style saree draping:

1. Pleat Formation: Start by tucking the plain end or the pallu (decorative end) of the saree into the waistband of your underskirt or petticoat, slightly to the right side of your navel. Leave a shorter length for the pallu on the right side.

2. Making Pleats: Take the loose end of the saree, known as the free end or the working end, and make about 5-7 pleats of approximately 5-6 inches each. Ensure that the pleats are even and face towards the left side.

3. Tucking Pleats: Hold the pleats together and tuck them into the waistband, slightly towards the left side. Adjust the length of the saree according to your comfort and the desired height of the hemline.

4. Pallu Placement: Bring the remaining portion of the saree, known as the pallu, over your left shoulder from the back to the front. Allow it to fall freely over your left arm, creating a graceful drape.

5. Pinning the Pallu: Use a decorative pin or brooch to secure the pallu in place on the left shoulder. You can

also pleat the pallu for a neater look or let it flow freely for a more casual appearance.

6. Final Adjustments: Ensure that the saree is draped evenly and smoothly, with the pleats neatly tucked and the pallu elegantly placed. Take a few steps and move your arms to ensure that the saree is comfortable and doesn't restrict your movements.

The Nivi style draping is known for its simplicity, sophistication, and versatility. It accentuates the curves of the body, creating a flattering silhouette. The pallu draped over the left shoulder adds an element of grace and charm to the overall look. This style is often preferred for formal occasions, weddings, festivals, and other special events in North Indian culture.

The Nivi style saree draping has been popularized through generations and continues to be a timeless and classic choice for women across North India. It allows for creativity in choosing different fabrics, colors, and patterns, making each saree drape unique. Whether it's a traditional silk saree, a lightweight chiffon saree, or a heavily embellished designer saree, the Nivi style enhances the beauty of the saree and complements the wearer's personality with elegance and poise.

Bengali style (distinctive draping style of Bengal)

The Bengali style of saree draping is a distinctive and traditional draping style that is specific to the Bengali culture. It is characterized by its unique pleat arrangement and the way the pallu (decorative end) is draped over the shoulder. Let's delve into the key features and steps involved in draping a saree in the Bengali style:

1. Tucking the Saree: Begin by tucking the plain end or the pallu of the saree into the waistband of your underskirt or petticoat, slightly to the right side of your navel. Leave a shorter length for the pallu on the right side.
2. Making Pleats: Take the loose end of the saree, known as the free end or the working end, and make 3-4 wide pleats of approximately 5-6 inches each. The pleats should be evenly sized and face towards the left side.
3. Tucking Pleats: Hold the pleats together and tuck them into the waistband, slightly towards the left side. Ensure that the pleats are neatly arranged and aligned.
4. Pallu Draping: Take the remaining portion of the saree, which is the pallu, and bring it from the back over your left shoulder to the front. Allow the pallu to fall freely over your left arm, forming loose pleats.
5. Keya-Aanchal: The distinctive feature of the Bengali style is the Keya-Aanchal, which refers to the way the pallu is pleated and pinned at the shoulder. Take the loose end of the pallu and bring it back to the front,

pleating it neatly. Pin it to the left shoulder using a decorative pin or brooch. The pleats create a fan-like appearance, adding elegance to the overall look.

6. Final Adjustments: Ensure that the saree is draped evenly and smoothly, with the pleats neatly tucked and the pallu gracefully arranged. Take a few steps and move your arms to ensure that the saree is comfortable and allows for easy movement.

The Bengali style saree draping is known for its grace, simplicity, and cultural significance. It is often adorned with traditional Bengali motifs and designs, reflecting the rich heritage of Bengal. This draping style is commonly worn during festive occasions, cultural events, and weddings in Bengal and is an integral part of Bengali women's attire.

The Bengali style of saree draping not only enhances the beauty of the saree but also showcases the wearer's pride in their culture and traditions. It is a symbol of elegance and grace, capturing the essence of Bengali aesthetics. Whether it's a traditional tant saree, a vibrant silk saree, or a handloom creation, draping the saree in the Bengali style adds a touch of sophistication and creates a distinct fashion statement.

Maharashtrian style (nauvari saree draping)

The Maharashtrian style of saree draping, also known as the Nauvari saree draping, is a unique and traditional draping style that originates from the state of Maharashtra in India. It is characterized by the distinct way the saree is draped to create a trouser-like appearance. Let's explore the key features and steps involved in draping a saree in the Maharashtrian style:

1. Preparing the Saree: Start by tucking the plain end of the saree (without the pallu) into the waistband of your underskirt or petticoat, ensuring that the saree is wrapped around your waist from right to left.
2. Creating Pleats: Take the remaining fabric of the saree and make around 4 to 5 pleats of approximately 5-6 inches each. Make sure the pleats are equal in size and fold them towards the left side.
3. Tying the Knot: Take the pleated portion of the saree and bring it between your legs towards the back. Tie a knot with the saree ends, securing it at the center of your waist. This knot forms the trouser-like appearance of the draping style.
4. Draping the Pallu: Now, take the loose end of the saree, which is the pallu, and bring it over your left shoulder from behind. Let the pallu fall freely over your left arm.
5. Pinning the Pallu: Take the loose end of the pallu and drape it across your chest, bringing it towards the back. Pin the pallu to the right shoulder using a safety pin or traditional brooch, ensuring that it stays in place.
6. Final Adjustments: Ensure that the saree is draped evenly and securely. Adjust the pleats and pallu as

needed to create a neat and elegant look. Take a few steps and move your arms to ensure that the saree allows for easy movement and comfort.

The Maharashtrian style of saree draping, or the Nauvari saree draping, is widely worn during traditional Maharashtrian festivals, cultural events, and weddings. It represents the rich cultural heritage of Maharashtra and showcases the pride and grace of Maharashtrian women.

The Nauvari saree is typically made of cotton or silk fabric and is adorned with traditional motifs and designs. It is a symbol of empowerment and strength, as it allows women to move freely and actively participate in various activities. The draping style adds a unique charm and elegance to the overall attire, making it a popular choice among Maharashtrian women.

Whether it's a festive celebration, a wedding ceremony, or a cultural gathering, draping a saree in the Maharashtrian style not only reflects the traditions and customs of Maharashtra but also highlights the beauty and grace of the wearer. It is a true representation of Maharashtrian culture and a fashion statement that captures the attention of all.

Tamilian style (Madisar and Pudavai draping)

The Tamilian style of saree draping is deeply rooted in the culture and traditions of Tamil Nadu, a state in South India. It is known for its unique draping techniques, namely the Madisar and Pudavai draping styles. Let's explore these two distinctive draping styles:

1. Madisar Draping: The Madisar is a traditional and elaborate draping style followed by married women, especially during auspicious occasions and religious ceremonies. Here are the key steps involved in draping a saree in the Madisar style:

     - Step 1: Begin by tucking the plain end of the saree (without the pallu) into the waistband of your underskirt or petticoat, ensuring that the saree is wrapped around your waist from right to left.

     - Step 2: Make approximately 6 to 9 pleats of equal width from the remaining fabric of the saree. The number of pleats may vary based on personal preference.

     - Step 3: Take the pleated portion and bring it around the waist from right to left, covering the tucked-in end. Secure it at the center of your waist with a knot.

     - Step 4: Drape the remaining fabric, which is the pallu, from the back over your right shoulder, and bring it towards the front, crossing it over your chest.

- Step 5: Take the pallu towards the back and tuck it into the waistband on the left side, allowing it to fall freely over your left shoulder.

2. Pudavai Draping: The Pudavai draping style is commonly followed by unmarried girls and younger women. It is a simpler draping style compared to the Madisar. Here are the key steps involved in draping a saree in the Pudavai style:

- Step 1: Start by tucking the plain end of the saree (without the pallu) into the waistband of your underskirt or petticoat, ensuring that the saree is wrapped around your waist from right to left.
- Step 2: Make approximately 4 to 5 pleats of equal width from the remaining fabric of the saree. The number of pleats may vary based on personal preference.
- Step 3: Bring the pleated portion to the front, between the legs, and tuck it into the waistband on the left side.
- Step 4: Drape the remaining fabric, which is the pallu, over your left shoulder from the back and let it fall freely over your left arm.

Both the Madisar and Pudavai draping styles showcase the rich cultural heritage of Tamil Nadu. These draping styles not only add grace and elegance to the saree but also reflect the customs and traditions followed by Tamilian women. The choice of saree fabric, colors, and designs may vary based on personal preferences and the occasion.

The Tamilian style of saree draping is a visual representation of the vibrant Tamil culture and an embodiment of the pride and identity of Tamil women. It has been passed down through generations, preserving the customs and values associated with it.

Whether it's a wedding, religious ceremony, or cultural event, draping a saree in the Tamilian style, be it the Madisar or Pudavai, is a way for women to connect with their roots, express their cultural identity, and radiate elegance. It is a celebration of the rich traditions and the timeless beauty of Tamil Nadu.

Gujarati style (seedha pallu and front pallu draping)

The Gujarati style of saree draping is a beautiful and distinctive draping style originating from the state of Gujarat in western India. Known for its vibrant colors, intricate designs, and unique draping techniques, Gujarati sarees and their draping styles are a reflection of the rich cultural heritage of the region. Let's explore two popular Gujarati draping styles: Seedha Pallu and Front Pallu.

1. Seedha Pallu Draping: The Seedha Pallu style is characterized by draping the pallu (decorative end) of the saree in a forward direction over the shoulder. Here are the key steps involved in draping a saree in the Seedha Pallu style:

   - Step 1: Begin by tucking the plain end of the saree (without the pallu) into the waistband of your underskirt or petticoat, ensuring that the saree is wrapped around your waist from right to left.
   - Step 2: Make approximately 5 to 7 pleats of equal width from the remaining fabric of the saree, starting from the tucked-in end.
   - Step 3: Take the pleated portion and bring it towards the front, crossing it over your chest.
   - Step 4: Drape the pallu over your left shoulder from the front, allowing it to fall gracefully over your left arm.
   - Step 5: Secure the pallu in place by pleating it

and tucking it into the waistband on the left side.

2. Front Pallu Draping: The Front Pallu style is characterized by draping the pallu of the saree in the front, covering the chest. It is often adorned with intricate designs and embellishments. Here are the key steps involved in draping a saree in the Front Pallu style:

- Step 1: Start by tucking the plain end of the saree (without the pallu) into the waistband of your underskirt or petticoat, ensuring that the saree is wrapped around your waist from right to left.
- Step 2: Make approximately 5 to 7 pleats of equal width from the remaining fabric of the saree, starting from the tucked-in end.
- Step 3: Take the pleated portion and bring it towards the front, crossing it over your chest.
- Step 4: Drape the pallu over your right shoulder from the front, allowing it to fall over your left arm and across your chest.
- Step 5: Bring the remaining portion of the pallu from behind and pleat it neatly, securing it at the back or tucking it into the waistband on the left side.

Both the Seedha Pallu and Front Pallu draping styles are known for their elegance and charm. They showcase the intricate details and vibrant colors of Gujarati sarees, capturing the essence of Gujarati culture and traditions. These draping styles are often adorned with heavy embroidery, mirror work, and embellishments, making them a visual delight.

Gujarati women embrace these draping styles during festivals, weddings, and other celebratory occasions, as well as in their day-to-day lives. The choice of saree fabric, designs, and colors may vary based on personal preferences and the significance of the event.

The Gujarati style of saree draping is a true reflection of the region's cultural richness, craftsmanship, and traditional values. It is not just a way of wearing a saree; it is an art form that celebrates the beauty of Gujarat and its people.

By embracing the Seedha Pallu and Front Pallu draping styles, women not only enhance their personal style but also pay homage to the vibrant heritage and traditions of Gujarat. The elegance and grace of these draping styles make Gujarati sarees a timeless fashion statement, cherished by women across generations.

Bridal sarees and wedding ensembles

Weddings are a momentous occasion in Indian culture, and the choice of attire for the bride holds immense significance. Bridal sarees are known for their opulence, intricate craftsmanship, and the ability to transform a bride into a vision of grace and beauty. Let's delve into the world of bridal sarees and wedding ensembles, which are a captivating blend of tradition, craftsmanship, and contemporary fashion.

1. Bridal Sarees: Bridal sarees are often crafted with the utmost care, using luxurious fabrics, intricate embellishments, and exquisite embroidery. These sarees are designed to make the bride the center of attention on her special day. Various regions in India have their own distinct styles of bridal sarees, each showcasing unique weaving techniques, motifs, and designs.

   - Banarasi Bridal Sarees: Banarasi sarees, known for their rich silk fabric and intricate zari work, are a popular choice for bridal wear. These sarees, handwoven in Varanasi, Uttar Pradesh, feature opulent brocades and intricate designs that add a regal touch to the bride's ensemble.
   - Kanjivaram Bridal Sarees: Kanjivaram sarees, originating from Tamil Nadu, are renowned for their lustrous silk fabric and vibrant colors. These sarees are characterized by their wide borders, intricate zari work, and traditional motifs, making them a preferred choice for South Indian brides.
   - Lehenga Sarees: Lehenga sarees combine the

elegance of a saree with the convenience of a lehenga. These ensembles feature a pre-stitched pleated skirt (lehenga) with a saree drape, creating a seamless blend of traditional and contemporary styles. Lehenga sarees often feature heavy embellishments, intricate embroidery, and intricate blouse designs.

2. Wedding Ensembles: Apart from bridal sarees, Indian weddings offer a plethora of other enchanting ensembles that complement the bride's overall look and add to the grandeur of the occasion.

- Lehengas: Lehengas are long, voluminous skirts paired with embellished blouses and dupattas (stoles). These ensembles are known for their ornate designs, intricate embroidery, and vibrant colors. Lehengas allow brides to exude elegance and grace as they make their way to the wedding ceremony.

- Anarkali Suits: Anarkali suits are floor-length outfits with a fitted bodice and a flared skirt. These suits feature intricate embroidery, delicate embellishments, and flowing fabrics. Anarkali suits offer a regal and feminine look, perfect for pre-wedding functions or receptions.

- Salwar Kameez: Salwar kameez is a versatile three-piece outfit consisting of a tunic-style top (kameez), loose-fitting trousers (salwar), and a dupatta. These ensembles are available in a wide range of designs, from simple and elegant to heavily embellished, allowing brides to choose a style that matches their preferences.

Bridal sarees and wedding ensembles are not merely garments; they are a reflection of the bride's personality, culture, and the rich traditions of India. They symbolize grace, beauty, and the beginning of a new chapter in a bride's life. The intricate craftsmanship, attention to detail, and the use of luxurious fabrics make these ensembles timeless and cherished heirlooms for generations to come.

Festive sarees

India is a land of vibrant festivals, where traditional attire plays a significant role in celebrations. Festive sarees hold a special place in these joyous occasions, adding a touch of elegance, color, and tradition to the festivities. Let's explore the world of festive sarees, which are a reflection of the rich cultural heritage and artistic brilliance of India.

1. Silk Sarees: Silk sarees are a popular choice for festivals, known for their luxurious texture, intricate designs, and lustrous appearance. Each region in India has its own signature silk saree, showcasing unique weaving techniques and motifs. Some of the well-known silk sarees for festivals include:

    - Kanjivaram Silk Sarees: Kanjivaram sarees, crafted in Tamil Nadu, are known for their rich silk fabric, vibrant colors, and intricate zari work. These sarees feature traditional motifs inspired by temple art and mythology, making them a perfect choice for auspicious occasions.
    - Banarasi Silk Sarees: Banarasi sarees from Varanasi, Uttar Pradesh, are renowned for their opulent brocade work and intricate designs. These sarees often feature gold and silver zari work, floral motifs, and intricate patterns, making them a symbol of grandeur and elegance.

2. Handloom Sarees: Handloom sarees are cherished for their authenticity, craftsmanship, and the use of natural fibers. These sarees are made using

traditional handloom techniques passed down through generations, making them a testament to the rich weaving heritage of India. Some popular handloom sarees for festivals include:

- Chanderi Sarees: Chanderi sarees, woven in Madhya Pradesh, are known for their lightweight texture and delicate motifs. These sarees often feature gold and silver zari work, butis (small motifs), and traditional patterns, making them a graceful choice for festive occasions.

- Maheshwari Sarees: Maheshwari sarees, hailing from Madhya Pradesh, are characterized by their distinctive border designs and contrasting colors. These sarees showcase a blend of cotton and silk yarns, creating a unique texture and drape. Maheshwari sarees are adorned with geometric patterns, stripes, and checks, adding a touch of contemporary flair to traditional festivities.

3. Embroidered Sarees: Festive sarees often feature exquisite embroidery work, enhancing their beauty and making them stand out. Different types of embroidery techniques are employed to create stunning patterns and motifs on the sarees. Some popular embroidered sarees for festivals include:

- Zardozi Sarees: Zardozi is a type of heavy embroidery done using gold and silver threads, along with precious stones and beads. Zardozi work adds a royal and regal touch to sarees, making them perfect for grand festivities and celebrations.

- Phulkari Sarees: Phulkari embroidery, originating from Punjab, involves vibrant thread work in floral patterns. Phulkari sarees are known for their colorful and eye-catching designs, making them a symbol of joy and happiness during festive occasions.

Festive sarees not only showcase the exquisite craftsmanship and artistic brilliance of Indian artisans but also provide a platform to celebrate and preserve the rich cultural heritage of the country. The vibrant colors, intricate designs, and the choice of fabrics make these sarees a true embodiment of elegance and tradition.

Office and formal wear sarees

Sarees are not only reserved for festive occasions and weddings but also find their place in professional settings as office and formal wear. These sarees strike a balance between elegance, professionalism, and comfort, allowing women to exude confidence and grace in their workplace. Let's explore some popular choices for office and formal wear sarees:

1. Cotton Sarees: Cotton sarees are a go-to option for office wear due to their lightweight and breathable nature. They offer comfort throughout the day and are easy to manage. With their subtle and understated designs, cotton sarees bring a touch of sophistication to the workplace. They are available in various styles like handloom cotton, Kota cotton, and Chettinad cotton, each representing the regional weaving traditions of India.

2. Linen Sarees: Linen sarees are another excellent choice for office and formal wear. Known for their crisp texture and refined appearance, linen sarees offer a contemporary and sophisticated look. They come in a range of colors and patterns, making them versatile for various professional settings.

3. Georgette Sarees: Georgette sarees are lightweight, flowy, and easy to drape, making them a popular choice for formal occasions. These sarees often feature minimalistic designs, delicate embellishments, and a subtle sheen, giving them an elegant and polished look. Georgette sarees are comfortable to wear for long hours and can be paired with formal blouses for a professional

appearance.

4. Silk Blends: Silk blend sarees strike a balance between the richness of silk and the comfort of other fabrics. They are a popular choice for formal occasions and office wear, offering a touch of sophistication and elegance. Silk blends like silk-cotton, silk-georgette, and silk-crepe create a beautiful drape while ensuring ease of movement.

5. Organza Sarees: Organza sarees are lightweight, sheer, and perfect for formal wear. These sarees often feature intricate embroidery, delicate prints, or subtle motifs, adding a touch of elegance to your office attire. The transparency of organza lends a contemporary and chic look, making it suitable for corporate environments.

6. Plain and Solid Colored Sarees: Sometimes, simplicity speaks volumes in a professional setting. Plain and solid colored sarees in subtle shades like pastels, neutrals, and earthy tones can create a sophisticated and refined look. These sarees provide a clean and polished appearance, allowing you to accessorize with statement jewelry or a contrasting blouse.

When it comes to office and formal wear sarees, comfort, professionalism, and personal style are key factors to consider. The choice of fabric, colors, and designs should align with the workplace culture while reflecting your individual taste. With the right selection, office and formal wear sarees can empower women, making them feel confident, stylish, and ready to conquer the professional world.

Casual and daily wear sarees

Sarees are not just reserved for special occasions and formal events but can also be a part of your everyday wardrobe. Casual and daily wear sarees offer comfort, ease of movement, and a touch of elegance for your regular activities. Let's explore some popular choices for casual and daily wear sarees:

1. Cotton Sarees: Cotton sarees are a timeless choice for daily wear. They are lightweight, breathable, and ideal for the Indian climate. Cotton sarees come in various weaves and designs, such as handloom cotton, Bengal cotton, and Chanderi cotton, offering a wide range of options to suit your style and preferences.

2. Linen Sarees: Linen sarees are known for their comfort and versatility. They are lightweight, absorbent, and perfect for everyday wear. Linen sarees come in a range of colors and textures, allowing you to experiment with different looks. They offer a casual yet elegant appearance and are suitable for both formal and informal settings.

3. Printed Sarees: Printed sarees are a popular choice for casual wear. They come in a variety of prints, such as floral, geometric, abstract, and ethnic motifs, adding vibrancy and charm to your daily attire. Printed sarees can be made of various fabrics like georgette, chiffon, or crepe, providing a lightweight and easy-to-manage option for regular wear.

4. Handloom Sarees: Handloom sarees showcase the rich weaving traditions of India and are a beautiful choice for daily wear. They are available in different regional

styles, such as Banarasi, Kanjivaram, and Maheshwari, each with its unique patterns and motifs. Handloom sarees offer a blend of comfort, durability, and elegance, making them suitable for everyday use.

5. Plain and Solid Colored Sarees: Sometimes, simplicity is the key to casual elegance. Plain and solid colored sarees in soothing hues like pastels, earthy tones, or neutrals can be versatile options for daily wear. They can be effortlessly paired with various blouses and accessories to create different looks.

6. Light Embellished Sarees: For those who prefer a touch of embellishment in their daily wear sarees, light embellished sarees are a great choice. These sarees feature minimalistic embroidery, sequins, or beadwork, adding subtle glamour to your everyday look without overwhelming it.

Casual and daily wear sarees are designed to offer comfort, ease, and style for your regular activities. They allow you to embrace the grace and elegance of sarees while going about your daily routine. Whether it's running errands, attending social gatherings, or simply enjoying your leisure time, casual and daily wear sarees can be your trusted companions, reflecting your personal style and enhancing your confidence.

Special occasion sarees (parties, receptions, etc.)

When it comes to special occasions like parties, receptions, weddings, and festive celebrations, sarees hold a special place in a woman's wardrobe. These occasions call for sarees that are glamorous, elegant, and make a statement. Let's explore some popular choices for special occasion sarees:

1. Silk Sarees: Silk sarees are synonymous with grandeur and are a go-to choice for special occasions. Whether it's the rich and opulent Banarasi silk, the exquisite Kanjivaram silk, the regal Mysore silk, or the elegant Patola silk, these sarees feature intricate patterns, vibrant colors, and luxurious textures. They instantly elevate your look and make you feel like a queen.

2. Designer Sarees: Designer sarees are crafted by renowned fashion designers, combining traditional craftsmanship with contemporary designs. These sarees feature unique patterns, innovative drapes, and intricate embellishments. They are often made with high-quality fabrics like georgette, chiffon, or net, adorned with embroidery, sequins, zari work, or stone embellishments. Designer sarees are perfect for making a fashion statement at special occasions.

3. Embroidered Sarees: Embroidered sarees add a touch of elegance and sophistication to your special occasion look. These sarees feature intricate embroidery work done by skilled artisans. The embroidery can be in

various styles, such as zardozi, thread work, mirror work, or stone work. Embroidered sarees come in a range of fabrics, including georgette, chiffon, net, and silk, and are available in a multitude of colors and designs.

4. Sequin and Beaded Sarees: If you want to sparkle and shine at special events, sequin and beaded sarees are the perfect choice. These sarees are embellished with sequins, beads, or crystals, creating a stunning effect under lights. They are available in various fabrics and designs, allowing you to choose the level of sparkle that suits your personal style.

5. Half and Half Sarees: Half and half sarees are a contemporary take on traditional sarees. They feature a combination of contrasting colors or fabrics, creating a visually striking look. The upper half and lower half of the saree may have different prints, colors, or embellishments, adding a modern twist to your special occasion attire.

6. Sarees with Unique Drapes: Special occasions are the perfect time to experiment with different draping styles. Drapes like the butterfly drape, lehenga-style drape, or the mermaid drape can give a unique and eye-catching look to your saree. These drapes require some practice, but they are sure to make you stand out from the crowd.

Special occasion sarees are designed to make you feel beautiful, confident, and ready to celebrate. They reflect the grandeur of the occasion and allow you to express your personal style in a captivating way.

Silk sarees

Silk sarees hold a special place in the world of sarees, renowned for their timeless elegance, exquisite craftsmanship, and luxurious feel. Made from silk fabric, these sarees are highly sought after for their rich textures, vibrant colors, and intricate designs. Let's delve into the enchanting world of silk sarees and explore their beauty and significance:

1. Kanjivaram Silk Sarees: Originating from the town of Kanchipuram in Tamil Nadu, Kanjivaram silk sarees are renowned for their opulence and intricate craftsmanship. These sarees are woven with pure silk threads and adorned with traditional motifs like peacocks, temple borders, and floral patterns. The lustrous sheen of the silk and the richness of the zari work make Kanjivaram sarees a symbol of grandeur and heritage.

2. Banarasi Silk Sarees: Hailing from the city of Varanasi in Uttar Pradesh, Banarasi silk sarees are known for their regal allure and fine craftsmanship. These sarees are woven with silk threads and enriched with intricate brocade designs, including motifs like floral patterns, paisleys, and Mughal-inspired designs. The heavy zari work and the luxurious feel of Banarasi silk make these sarees a popular choice for weddings and festive occasions.

3. Mysore Silk Sarees: Originating from the city of Mysore in Karnataka, Mysore silk sarees are known for their simplicity and elegance. These sarees feature a soft and lightweight silk fabric with minimalistic designs. They

often showcase bold and contrasting borders, making them perfect for both casual and formal occasions. Mysore silk sarees are favored for their comfort and graceful draping.

4. Patola Silk Sarees: Hailing from the state of Gujarat, Patola silk sarees are famous for their vibrant colors and intricate double ikat weaving technique. These sarees are handwoven by skilled artisans, where the yarn is dyed before weaving to create symmetrical patterns on both sides of the fabric. Patola silk sarees are a testament to the impeccable craftsmanship and artistry of the weavers.

5. Baluchari Silk Sarees: Originating from the region of West Bengal, Baluchari silk sarees are known for their intricate and storytelling designs. These sarees feature elaborate silk thread motifs depicting scenes from epics like Ramayana and Mahabharata. The detailed weaving and the use of rich colors make Baluchari silk sarees a cherished piece of art.

Silk sarees are not just garments; they are a celebration of culture, tradition, and the masterful skills of artisans. They are passed down through generations as heirlooms and are worn on auspicious occasions to signify grace, beauty, and elegance.

Cotton sarees

Cotton sarees are beloved for their comfort, versatility, and breathability, making them a popular choice for everyday wear, casual occasions, and summer seasons. These sarees are made from soft and lightweight cotton fabric, which is known for its ability to keep the body cool and comfortable in hot climates. Let's explore the world of cotton sarees and discover their charm and significance:

1. Chanderi Cotton Sarees: Originating from the town of Chanderi in Madhya Pradesh, Chanderi cotton sarees are renowned for their sheer texture and delicate handwoven motifs. These sarees often feature intricate gold or silver zari borders and butis (small motifs) spread across the fabric. Chanderi cotton sarees strike a perfect balance between elegance and simplicity, making them suitable for both formal and casual occasions.

2. Maheshwari Cotton Sarees: Hailing from the town of Maheshwar in Madhya Pradesh, Maheshwari cotton sarees are known for their unique and eye-catching designs. These sarees feature a blend of cotton and silk threads, resulting in a lightweight yet lustrous fabric. Maheshwari sarees are characterized by their vibrant colors, contrasting borders, and intricate motifs like stripes, checks, and floral patterns.

3. Tant Cotton Sarees: Popular in West Bengal, tant cotton sarees are cherished for their simplicity and comfort. Made from fine handwoven cotton, these sarees are light and airy, perfect for hot and humid climates. Tant sarees

often feature wide borders and intricate threadwork in contrasting colors. They are known for their vibrant hues and subtle elegance, making them a staple in Bengali culture.

4. Kota Doria Cotton Sarees: Originating from Kota in Rajasthan, Kota Doria cotton sarees are admired for their sheer and translucent texture. These sarees are woven with a blend of cotton and silk threads, resulting in a fabric that is lightweight, breathable, and easy to drape. Kota Doria sarees are known for their square-shaped patterns called khats, which are created using traditional weaving techniques.

5. Handloom Cotton Sarees: Handloom cotton sarees come in a variety of regional styles and designs, showcasing the rich textile heritage of India. These sarees are handwoven by skilled artisans using traditional techniques, resulting in unique patterns, textures, and motifs. Handloom cotton sarees celebrate the craftsmanship of weavers and highlight the beauty of natural cotton fibers.

Cotton sarees are not only comfortable and practical but also showcase the diverse weaving traditions and artistry of India. They are a reflection of the country's rich cultural heritage and are favored by women of all ages.

Georgette, chiffon, and crepe sarees

Georgette, chiffon, and crepe sarees are renowned for their lightweight, flowy, and graceful nature. These sarees are favored for their elegant drape, subtle sheen, and versatility. Let's explore the distinct characteristics and allure of georgette, chiffon, and crepe sarees:

1. Georgette Sarees: Georgette is a sheer and lightweight fabric known for its crinkled texture. Georgette sarees are admired for their fluid drape and soft feel. These sarees are often made from synthetic fibers like polyester or silk-blended georgette. Georgette sarees come in a wide range of colors, prints, and embellishments, making them suitable for both formal and festive occasions. They exude a graceful and feminine charm that adds an element of sophistication to any ensemble.

2. Chiffon Sarees: Chiffon is a lightweight and translucent fabric that is highly prized for its delicate appearance and soft texture. Chiffon sarees are known for their ethereal beauty and effortless drape. These sarees are made from synthetic fibers like polyester or silk-blended chiffon, offering a comfortable and breathable wearing experience. Chiffon sarees often feature intricate embroidery, sequins, or embellishments, making them a popular choice for parties, weddings, and special occasions. They impart a sense of elegance and grace to the wearer.

3. Crepe Sarees: Crepe is a fabric known for its subtle texture and crisp drape. Crepe sarees are characterized

by their slightly grainy surface and lightweight nature. These sarees can be made from various materials, including silk, polyester, or a blend of both. Crepe sarees come in a variety of styles, ranging from simple and understated to heavily embellished designs. They are admired for their versatility, making them suitable for both formal and casual events. Crepe sarees offer a sleek and sophisticated look with a touch of modernity.

Georgette, chiffon, and crepe sarees are popular choices for women who seek comfort, elegance, and a touch of glamour in their attire. These sarees are known for their breezy feel, effortless draping, and ability to accentuate the feminine silhouette.

Embroidery, zari work, and embellishments

Embroidery, zari work, and embellishments are integral elements of saree craftsmanship that add intricate beauty and enhance the overall appeal of a saree. These artistic techniques involve the use of threads, metallic threads (zari), and decorative elements to create stunning patterns, motifs, and designs on the saree fabric. Let's explore the significance and variations of embroidery, zari work, and embellishments in sarees:

1. Embroidery: Embroidery is the art of decorating fabric with needle and thread. It involves creating intricate designs, patterns, and motifs using various stitches and techniques. Embroidery on sarees can be done with silk threads, cotton threads, metallic threads, or a combination of these. The types of embroidery commonly seen on sarees include zardozi, kantha, mirror work, chikankari, and thread work, among others. Embroidery adds depth, texture, and visual interest to the saree, elevating its aesthetic appeal and making it a statement piece.

2. Zari Work: Zari work refers to the use of metallic threads, typically gold or silver, in saree embellishments. Zari threads are intricately woven into the fabric, creating beautiful patterns, borders, and motifs. Zari work is often seen in traditional and bridal sarees, adding a touch of opulence, grandeur, and traditional charm. It imparts a shimmering effect to the saree, making it perfect for special occasions and festivities.

3. Embellishments: Sarees are often adorned with various

embellishments to enhance their beauty and make them stand out. These embellishments can include sequins, beads, stones, pearls, mirrors, and crystals. They are meticulously handcrafted or intricately woven into the saree fabric, creating eye-catching designs and adding a touch of glamour and sparkle. Embellishments can be used sparingly for a subtle effect or lavishly for a more dramatic look, depending on the style and occasion.

Embroidery, zari work, and embellishments are exquisite details that showcase the skill, artistry, and cultural heritage associated with saree making. They bring life and character to the fabric, transforming a simple saree into a work of art.

Saree borders and motifs

Borders and motifs play a significant role in defining the aesthetic appeal and regional identity of a saree. They are intricately woven or embroidered elements that adorn the edges and body of the saree, adding charm, elegance, and cultural significance. Let's explore the different types of saree borders and motifs:

1. Borders: Saree borders are decorative elements that frame the edges of the saree. They can be wide or narrow, plain or embellished, and often feature unique patterns and designs. Some popular types of saree borders include:

    - Zari Border: Zari borders are made using metallic threads, typically gold or silver, and are known for their shimmering effect. They add a touch of opulence and grandeur to the saree.

    - Contrast Border: Contrast borders are created using a different color or pattern than the main body of the saree. They provide a striking contrast and highlight the beauty of the saree.

    - Embroidered Border: Embroidered borders feature intricate thread work or embellishments along the edges of the saree. They can showcase various embroidery styles, such as zardozi, kantha, or mirror work.

    - Lace Border: Lace borders are delicate and intricately patterned fabric trims that are attached to the edges of the saree. They add a feminine and elegant touch to the overall look.

2. Motifs: Motifs are decorative patterns or designs that are woven or printed onto the body of the saree. They often hold cultural or symbolic significance and are representative of the region or community they belong to. Some popular motifs seen in sarees include:

  - Floral Motifs: Floral motifs are widely used in saree designs and represent beauty, nature, and femininity. They can range from delicate flowers to intricate floral patterns.
  - Paisley Motifs: Paisley motifs, also known as buta or mango motifs, are teardrop-shaped designs that symbolize fertility, prosperity, and life. They are commonly found in traditional and ethnic sarees.
  - Animal Motifs: Sarees often feature motifs of animals like peacocks, elephants, birds, or fish, which hold cultural or religious significance. These motifs add a touch of whimsy and charm to the saree.
  - Geometric Motifs: Geometric patterns and motifs are characterized by lines, shapes, and repetitive designs. They can be simple or intricate, creating a visually appealing pattern on the saree.

Borders and motifs are essential elements that contribute to the beauty, storytelling, and regional identity of sarees.

Blouse designs and trends

The blouse is an integral part of the saree ensemble, and its design and style can significantly impact the overall look of the outfit. Over the years, blouse designs have evolved, showcasing innovation, creativity, and a blend of traditional and contemporary elements. Let's explore some popular blouse designs and trends:

1. Classic Round Neck: The classic round neck blouse is a timeless design that suits various saree styles. It features a round neckline, providing a simple and elegant look. This versatile design can be paired with both traditional and modern sarees.

2. V-Neck Blouse: The V-neck blouse features a V-shaped neckline, which adds a touch of femininity and sophistication to the saree. It is a popular choice for sarees with heavy embroidery or work on the pallu, as it accentuates the overall look.

3. Halter Neck Blouse: The halter neck blouse has a high neckline that wraps around the neck, leaving the shoulders bare. It offers a modern and chic look, perfect for parties and special occasions. It pairs well with sarees that have minimal embellishments.

4. Backless Blouse: Backless blouses are trendy and glamorous, with a focus on showcasing the back. They feature intricate back designs, such as criss-cross patterns, cutouts, or tie-ups. Backless blouses add a sensual and stylish touch to the saree ensemble.

5. Off-Shoulder Blouse: Off-shoulder blouses are a modern and fashionable choice for sarees. They feature a

neckline that rests below the shoulders, exposing the collarbones and shoulders. Off-shoulder blouses add a contemporary flair to traditional sarees.

6. Sheer and Net Blouse: Sheer and net blouses are designed with translucent or see-through fabric, creating an ethereal and delicate look. They are often adorned with embroidery, sequins, or lace, adding a touch of elegance and glamour.

7. Elbow-Length Sleeves: Elbow-length sleeves are a popular choice for blouses as they provide a balance between coverage and style. They offer a modest yet trendy look, suitable for various occasions.

8. Bell Sleeves: Bell sleeves are characterized by their flared shape, resembling the shape of a bell. They add a dramatic and bohemian touch to the saree ensemble, making it a statement piece.

9. Statement Necklines: Blouses with statement necklines, such as boat neck, square neck, or sweetheart neck, are in vogue. They draw attention to the neckline and can be adorned with intricate embroidery, beading, or embellishments.

10. Cutwork and Embroidery: Blouses with cutwork detailing or elaborate embroidery are popular for adding intricacy and charm to the saree ensemble. These designs showcase craftsmanship and attention to detail.

Blouse designs and trends are ever-evolving, reflecting the dynamic fashion landscape and individual preferences.

Saree jewelry and accessories

When it comes to completing the perfect saree look, jewelry and accessories play a vital role. They add a touch of elegance, sophistication, and cultural significance to the overall ensemble. Let's explore some popular saree jewelry and accessories:

1. Necklaces: Necklaces are a staple accessory for sarees. They come in various designs, lengths, and materials, allowing you to choose the one that complements your saree. Traditional options include gold or silver necklaces with intricate designs, while contemporary choices may include statement necklaces or beaded strands.
2. Earrings: Earrings are an essential part of saree jewelry. They come in a wide range of styles, from delicate studs to elaborate jhumkas (chandelier earrings). Earrings can be chosen to match the necklace or stand out on their own, depending on the desired look.
3. Bangles and Bracelets: Bangles and bracelets add a touch of glamour to the hands and wrists. They can be made of gold, silver, or other materials, and may feature intricate designs, gemstones, or enamel work. Stack multiple bangles or wear a single statement bracelet to enhance your saree look.
4. Maang Tikka: The maang tikka is a traditional hair accessory that adorns the center of the forehead. It consists of a pendant that hangs on the forehead with an attached chain or string. Maang tikkas are available in various styles, including traditional designs with intricate embellishments or contemporary variations

with minimalist aesthetics.

5. Waist Belts: Waist belts, also known as kamarbandhs or kamarpati, are worn around the waist to enhance the silhouette and add a decorative element to the saree. They are often made of metal, such as gold or silver, and feature intricate designs or gemstone embellishments.

6. Nose Rings: Nose rings, or nath, are a traditional accessory worn by many Indian women with sarees. They come in different sizes and designs, ranging from simple studs to elaborate hoops with chains that connect to the ear.

7. Anklets: Anklets, also called payals or paayals, are worn around the ankles and create a pleasant jingling sound as you walk. They can be made of silver or gold and are often adorned with small bells or intricate charms.

8. Hair Accessories: Adorning the hair with accessories like hairpins, hair combs, or embellished clips can add a touch of elegance to your saree look. Choose accessories that match the style and color scheme of your saree.

9. Handbags and Clutches: A stylish handbag or clutch is a practical and fashionable accessory to carry with your saree. Opt for designs that complement the color and style of your attire.

10. Footwear: Completing your saree look with the right footwear is essential. Opt for comfortable yet stylish options like sandals, heels, or traditional footwear like juttis or mojaris.

Saree jewelry and accessories allow you to personalize your saree ensemble, showcasing your unique style and enhancing the beauty of the six-yard wonder.

Hairstyles and makeup to complement sarees

Choosing the right hairstyle and makeup can enhance your overall look when wearing a saree. Here are some popular hairstyles and makeup tips to complement sarees:

Hairstyles:

1. Traditional Bun: A classic choice, the traditional bun is a versatile hairstyle that goes well with all types of sarees. It keeps the focus on the saree and allows you to showcase intricate blouse designs or statement jewelry.
2. Side-Swept Curls: Soft, side-swept curls add a touch of glamour and elegance to your saree look. This hairstyle works well with both traditional and contemporary sarees, adding a romantic and feminine touch.
3. Half-Up, Half-Down: For a more modern and casual look, try a half-up, half-down hairstyle. This style keeps your hair off your face while still allowing some loose locks to frame your face.
4. Braided Hairstyles: Braids are a versatile option that can be styled in various ways. You can opt for a simple side braid, a fishtail braid, or a braided updo to add an intricate and stylish element to your saree look.

Makeup:

1. Natural and Dewy: Opt for a natural and dewy makeup look that enhances your features without overpowering the saree. Use a lightweight foundation, subtle blush, and a touch of highlighter for a fresh and radiant appearance.

2. Smoky Eyes: Smoky eyes can add drama and intensity to your saree look, especially for evening events. Pair it with a neutral lip color to balance the overall makeup.

3. Bold Lips: If you want to make a statement, choose a bold lip color that complements the colors of your saree. A vibrant red, deep plum, or rich berry shade can add a pop of color and elevate your look.

4. Winged Eyeliner: Winged eyeliner is a classic choice that adds definition and a touch of glamour to your eyes. Pair it with neutral eyeshadow shades for a timeless look.

5. Soft and Rosy: A soft and rosy makeup look is perfect for daytime events. Use soft pink or peach tones on your cheeks, lips, and eyes to achieve a fresh and youthful appearance.

6. Glitter and Shimmer: For special occasions and festive sarees, consider incorporating glitter or shimmer into your makeup look. Apply it sparingly on your eyelids or as a highlighter to add sparkle and glamour.

Remember to choose a hairstyle and makeup look that complements the overall style of your saree and aligns with the occasion. Experiment with different styles to find what suits you best, and don't forget to accessorize your hair with hairpins, flowers, or other decorative elements that coordinate with your saree.

Saree draping hacks and tips

Draping a saree can be a beautiful and elegant process, but it may take some practice to perfect. Here are some saree draping hacks and tips to help you achieve a flawless drape:

1. Invest in a well-fitted blouse: A properly fitted blouse is essential for a neat and well-draped saree. Ensure that your blouse fits well and complements your body shape, as it provides the foundation for the saree drape.

2. Use safety pins strategically: Safety pins can be your best friend when it comes to securing the pleats and pallu of your saree. Use small, discreet safety pins to hold the pleats in place and prevent them from shifting or coming undone.

3. Start with pleats: Begin by making the pleats at the front of the saree. Aim for around 5-7 pleats, depending on the width of the fabric and your personal preference. Make sure the pleats are even and well-aligned before tucking them into your waistband.

4. Secure the pallu: After securing the pleats, bring the loose end of the saree (the pallu) over your shoulder and let it hang freely. Use a safety pin to secure the pallu to your blouse, ensuring it stays in place.

5. Adjust the length: Check the length of your saree and make sure it's appropriate for your height. You can adjust the length by folding the saree at the bottom to achieve the desired look.

6. Practice pleat formation: Creating neat and even pleats is key to a well-draped saree. Practice folding the fabric and forming pleats before draping the saree to ensure

they are consistent and well-defined.

7. Use a saree belt or tuck in the pleats: To keep the pleats in place and prevent them from sagging or coming undone, you can use a saree belt or tuck the pleats firmly into your waistband.

8. Experiment with different draping styles: Don't be afraid to explore different draping styles and variations to find what suits you best. Each region in India has its own unique draping style, so you can try out different techniques and adapt them to your preference.

9. Pay attention to the pallu: The way you drape and style the pallu can significantly impact the overall look of your saree. You can experiment with different ways of pleating or pleat-free styles to add a touch of uniqueness to your drape.

10. Practice and seek assistance: Draping a saree takes practice, so don't get discouraged if it doesn't come out perfectly the first few times. Seek assistance from experienced individuals or watch online tutorials to learn different draping techniques and refine your skills.

Remember, confidence is key when wearing a saree. Embrace the grace and elegance of this traditional garment, and enjoy the process of draping it to create a stunning and personalized look. With practice and a few tricks up your sleeve, you'll become a pro at saree draping in no time.

Cleaning and washing sarees

Sarees are delicate garments that require special care when it comes to cleaning and washing. Here are some tips to help you keep your sarees clean and well-maintained:

1. Read the care instructions: Before cleaning your saree, always check the care instructions provided by the manufacturer. Different fabrics and embellishments may require specific cleaning methods, so it's important to follow the recommended guidelines.

2. Dry clean for delicate and heavily embellished sarees: If your saree is made of delicate fabrics like silk, chiffon, or has intricate embellishments like zari work or sequins, it's best to take it to a professional dry cleaner. They have the expertise to handle delicate fabrics and preserve the saree's quality.

3. Hand wash for cotton and synthetic sarees: Cotton and synthetic sarees can generally be hand washed at home. Fill a basin or sink with cold or lukewarm water and add a mild detergent suitable for delicate fabrics. Gently swirl the saree in the water, paying attention to any stained areas. Avoid rubbing or scrubbing vigorously, as it may damage the fabric. Rinse the saree thoroughly and squeeze out excess water gently.

4. Avoid soaking for long periods: It's important to avoid soaking your sarees for extended periods, as it may lead to color bleeding or fabric damage. Soak the saree for a maximum of 10-15 minutes and then proceed with the washing process.

5. Separate colors: When washing multiple sarees,

especially if they have different colors, it's important to separate them to prevent color transfer. Wash similar-colored sarees together or individually to avoid any discoloration.

6. Use gentle detergents: Opt for mild, gentle detergents specifically designed for delicate fabrics. Harsh detergents or bleach can damage the fabric or fade the colors of your saree. Follow the instructions on the detergent packaging for the appropriate amount to use.

7. Avoid wringing or twisting: After washing, gently squeeze out excess water from the saree without wringing or twisting it. Twisting or wringing can damage the fabric and cause it to lose its shape.

8. Drying the saree: Hang the saree to dry in a well-ventilated area away from direct sunlight. Avoid hanging it in a way that puts excessive strain on the fabric, such as using clothespins on the delicate areas. If necessary, use a padded hanger or drape the saree over a clean, smooth surface to dry.

9. Ironing: Once the saree is dry, you can iron it at a low or medium temperature setting. If your saree has intricate embellishments or delicate embroidery, it's advisable to use a protective cloth or iron the saree inside out to prevent any damage.

10. Storage: Store your sarees in a clean, dry place, away from moisture and direct sunlight. Fold them neatly and place them in a saree bag or wrap them in a cotton cloth to protect them from dust and insects.

Remember, it's essential to handle your sarees with care during the cleaning process to preserve their beauty and longevity. If you're unsure about cleaning a particular saree, it's always best to consult a professional or follow the instructions provided by the manufacturer.

Storing sarees properly

Proper storage of sarees is essential to maintain their quality and prevent damage. Here are some tips for storing sarees:

1. Clean and dry: Before storing your sarees, ensure they are clean and completely dry. Any dirt or moisture left on the fabric can lead to stains, mold, or mildew.

2. Fold carefully: Fold each saree neatly to avoid creases and wrinkles. Start by folding the saree lengthwise into a long strip. Then, fold it horizontally into smaller sections, making sure the borders and pallu (the decorative end) are visible. Avoid folding too tightly to prevent permanent creasing.

3. Use acid-free tissue paper: Place acid-free tissue paper between each fold to protect the saree from color transfer and creasing. The tissue paper acts as a barrier and helps maintain the fabric's integrity.

4. Store in breathable containers: Choose storage containers that allow for air circulation. Avoid using plastic bags or airtight containers, as they can trap moisture and lead to mold or mildew. Instead, opt for cotton saree bags or fabric storage boxes that provide a breathable environment for your sarees.

5. Avoid hanging for long periods: While it's common to hang sarees for display or short-term storage, long-term hanging can strain the fabric and cause it to lose its shape. If you need to hang sarees, use padded hangers to prevent any damage and minimize stress on the fabric.

6. Store in a cool, dry place: Find a cool, dry area to store your sarees. Avoid areas prone to excessive humidity or

temperature fluctuations, as they can affect the fabric's condition. Ideally, store them in a closet or wardrobe away from direct sunlight.

7. Rotate sarees periodically: To prevent fabric deterioration and discoloration, it's advisable to rotate your sarees periodically. This helps distribute the weight and exposure to light evenly, preserving the sarees' quality.

8. Check periodically: Occasionally inspect your stored sarees for any signs of pests, moisture, or damage. If you notice any issues, address them promptly to prevent further damage.

9. Maintain proper ventilation: Ensure the storage area has adequate ventilation to prevent the buildup of moisture or musty odors. You can place moisture-absorbing packets or silica gel packets in the storage containers to control humidity.

10. Store with care: Handle your stored sarees with care to avoid unnecessary creasing or mishandling. Whenever you retrieve a saree from storage, unfold it gently and give it some time to rest and regain its natural shape before wearing it.

By following these storage tips, you can keep your sarees in excellent condition, ensuring they remain vibrant and beautiful for years to come.

Preservation and restoration of vintage sarees

Preserving and restoring vintage sarees requires special care to maintain their beauty and historical value. Here are some tips for preserving and restoring vintage sarees:

1. Gentle cleaning: Before attempting any restoration, clean the saree gently to remove any dirt or stains. It's advisable to consult a professional textile conservator or a dry cleaner experienced in handling vintage textiles. They can use specialized techniques and mild cleaning agents to ensure the fabric's integrity is maintained.

2. Avoid harsh chemicals: Harsh cleaning chemicals can damage delicate vintage fabrics. Opt for gentle, pH-neutral cleansers specifically designed for textiles. Always spot test any cleaning solution on a small, inconspicuous area of the saree to ensure it doesn't cause any adverse reactions.

3. Repair tears and holes: Vintage sarees may have tears, holes, or loose threads. Seek the assistance of a professional textile conservator or a skilled tailor experienced in working with delicate fabrics. They can mend tears, reinforce weak areas, and secure loose threads using appropriate stitching techniques and matching threads.

4. Handle with care: When handling vintage sarees, be gentle and avoid pulling or tugging on the fabric. Support the weight of the saree with both hands to minimize stress on the delicate fibers.

5. Store in archival materials: Use acid-free tissue paper or unbleached cotton fabric to wrap and protect vintage

sarees during storage. Acid-free tissue paper helps prevent color transfer and provides a protective barrier between folds. Avoid using plastic bags or containers that can trap moisture.

6. Maintain proper humidity and temperature: Store vintage sarees in a controlled environment with moderate humidity and stable temperatures. Extremes in humidity and temperature can accelerate deterioration. Aim for a humidity level of around 50% and a temperature between 60 to 70 degrees Fahrenheit (15 to 21 degrees Celsius).

7. Avoid exposure to light: Protect vintage sarees from prolonged exposure to direct sunlight or harsh artificial light, as it can cause fading and discoloration. If displaying the saree, use UV-filtering glass or acrylic frames to shield it from harmful light.

8. Periodic inspection and maintenance: Regularly inspect stored vintage sarees for any signs of pests, mold, or deterioration. Check for loose threads, weak areas, or any other potential issues. Address any problems promptly to prevent further damage.

9. Seek professional assistance: If your vintage saree requires extensive restoration or conservation work, it's advisable to consult a professional textile conservator. They have the expertise and specialized tools to handle delicate fabrics and implement appropriate restoration techniques.

Remember, proper preservation and restoration techniques can help prolong the life of vintage sarees and ensure their cultural and historical significance is preserved for future generations to appreciate.

Artisans and weavers behind saree production

The production of sarees involves the skilled craftsmanship of numerous artisans and weavers who play a crucial role in preserving the rich tradition and heritage associated with these garments. These talented individuals contribute their expertise and artistry at various stages of the saree production process. Here are some key artisans and weavers involved:

1. Weavers: Weavers are at the heart of saree production. They are highly skilled in the art of handloom weaving, using traditional techniques that have been passed down through generations. Weavers meticulously create intricate patterns and designs on the loom, bringing the saree to life. They work with different types of yarns and threads, carefully interlacing them to create the desired fabric and motifs.

2. Dyers: Dyers are responsible for adding vibrant colors to the sarees. They possess extensive knowledge of natural and synthetic dyes, as well as the techniques required to achieve various shades and hues. Dyers use their expertise to dye the yarns or the woven fabric, carefully selecting the appropriate dyes and ensuring uniform color distribution.

3. Embroiderers: Embroiderers specialize in embellishing sarees with intricate and beautiful embroidery work. They skillfully hand-stitch intricate patterns using threads, beads, sequins, and other decorative elements. Embroiderers bring a touch of artistry and elegance to the saree, adding depth and texture to the overall design.

4. Block printers: Block printing is a traditional technique used to create unique patterns and motifs on sarees. Block printers carve intricate designs onto wooden blocks, which are then dipped in dye and pressed onto the fabric. This process is repeated meticulously to create a repeating pattern across the saree. Block printers contribute their expertise in creating visually appealing and culturally significant designs.

5. Designers: Designers play a vital role in saree production by conceptualizing and creating innovative designs. They collaborate closely with weavers, dyers, embroiderers, and other artisans to develop unique patterns, color combinations, and contemporary styles while respecting the traditional elements of saree design. Designers bring a fresh perspective and creative vision to the saree-making process.

6. Artistic communities and cooperatives: Many sarees are produced by artisan communities and cooperatives that bring together multiple skilled individuals. These communities serve as hubs for knowledge sharing, skill development, and collective production. They provide a platform for artisans to showcase their work, collaborate, and preserve traditional techniques.

The contributions of these artisans and weavers are essential in creating exquisite sarees that reflect the cultural diversity and artistic heritage of various regions. Their craftsmanship, attention to detail, and dedication ensure that each saree is a masterpiece of art and culture. Supporting these artisans not only promotes the rich heritage of sarees but also sustains their livelihoods and the traditional craft ecosystem.

Promoting handloom and sustainable saree practices

Promoting handloom and sustainable saree practices is crucial for the preservation of traditional craftsmanship, supporting artisans, and fostering sustainable and ethical fashion. Here are some key strategies to promote handloom and sustainable saree practices:

1. Education and Awareness: Raise awareness among consumers about the importance of handloom sarees and the artisans behind them. Educate people about the environmental and social impact of fast fashion and the benefits of choosing handloom sarees. Highlight the cultural significance and unique qualities of handloom sarees, emphasizing their sustainable and ethical aspects.

2. Collaboration and Support: Encourage collaborations between designers, artisans, and weavers to create contemporary designs that appeal to a wider audience while preserving traditional techniques. Provide support and resources to weaver communities, such as access to training, infrastructure, and fair trade practices. Collaborate with organizations and initiatives that promote handloom and sustainable fashion.

3. Ethical Sourcing and Supply Chains: Emphasize the importance of transparent and ethical sourcing practices. Encourage retailers and brands to source sarees directly from weaver communities, ensuring fair wages and working conditions. Promote transparency

in the supply chain and the traceability of materials.

4. Sustainable Materials and Processes: Encourage the use of sustainable materials such as organic cotton, natural dyes, and eco-friendly fibers in saree production. Promote the adoption of eco-friendly processes that minimize water and energy consumption, reduce waste, and prioritize environmentally friendly practices.

5. Consumer Education: Educate consumers about the benefits of choosing handloom sarees, including their durability, quality, and positive impact on communities and the environment. Share stories and information about the artisans and their craft to create a deeper connection between the saree and the consumer.

6. Events and Exhibitions: Organize events, exhibitions, and fashion shows dedicated to handloom sarees, showcasing the craftsmanship and diversity of designs. Provide platforms for artisans to showcase their work directly to consumers, building appreciation for handloom sarees and encouraging their purchase.

7. Policy Support: Advocate for supportive policies at the government level to protect and promote handloom industries. Encourage policies that provide financial support, skill development programs, and infrastructure development for artisans and weaver communities.

By actively promoting handloom and sustainable saree practices, we can contribute to the preservation of traditional craftsmanship, support the livelihoods of artisans, and create a more sustainable and ethical fashion ecosystem. It is through our collective efforts that we can ensure the continued existence and celebration of handloom sarees for generations to come.

Impact of globalization on the saree industry

Globalization has had a significant impact on the saree industry, bringing both opportunities and challenges. Here are some key aspects of globalization's impact on the saree industry:

1. Market Expansion: Globalization has opened up new markets and increased the reach of sarees beyond traditional boundaries. Sarees are now accessible to a global customer base through online platforms, international exhibitions, and cultural exchanges. This expanded market has provided opportunities for artisans and weavers to showcase their craft and generate higher demand for their products.

2. Cultural Exchange and Fusion: Globalization has led to cultural exchange and fusion in fashion trends. As sarees gain popularity worldwide, there is a growing interest in incorporating elements of saree draping and designs into global fashion styles. This cross-cultural influence has given rise to innovative interpretations of sarees, blending traditional motifs with contemporary aesthetics.

3. Technological Advancements: Globalization has facilitated the adoption of advanced technologies in the saree industry. Weavers now have access to modern equipment, digital design tools, and online platforms for marketing and sales. These technological advancements have improved production efficiency, expanded design possibilities, and enhanced the overall competitiveness of the saree industry.

4. Supply Chain Challenges: Globalization has brought

challenges in the supply chain of sarees. Increased demand for sarees has led to outsourcing and mass production, which sometimes compromises the authenticity and quality of handloom sarees. Moreover, competition from cheaper, machine-made imitations and fast fashion has put pressure on traditional handloom weavers.

5. Economic Opportunities: Globalization has provided economic opportunities for artisans and weavers in the saree industry. Increased demand for handloom sarees in international markets has led to better income prospects for weaver communities. Artisans now have the opportunity to directly connect with global customers, eliminating intermediaries and improving their economic prospects.

6. Preservation of Traditional Craftsmanship: Globalization has brought attention to the rich heritage and intricate craftsmanship of sarees. As sarees gain global recognition, there is a renewed interest in preserving traditional weaving techniques and supporting the livelihoods of artisans. Global appreciation for sarees has created a market for authentic, handmade products, incentivizing artisans to continue their craft and pass it on to future generations.

In summary, globalization has both positive and negative impacts on the saree industry. While it has expanded market opportunities and cultural exchange, it has also posed challenges such as increased competition and the need to maintain authenticity in the face of mass production. Balancing the benefits of globalization with the preservation of traditional craftsmanship is crucial for the sustainable growth of the saree industry in a globalized world.

Contemporary saree designers and their contributions

Contemporary saree designers have made significant contributions to the saree industry by infusing fresh ideas, innovative designs, and modern aesthetics into this traditional garment. Here are some renowned contemporary saree designers and their notable contributions:

1. Sabyasachi Mukherjee: Sabyasachi is known for his exquisite and opulent saree designs that blend traditional craftsmanship with contemporary sensibilities. His creations often feature intricate hand embroidery, rich fabrics, and a fusion of regional textiles. Sabyasachi's work has played a crucial role in popularizing sarees among the younger generation and showcasing the diversity of Indian textiles.

2. Anamika Khanna: Anamika Khanna is celebrated for her unconventional and experimental approach to saree design. She is known for blending traditional and modern elements, such as pairing sarees with unconventional blouses, incorporating unique draping techniques, and combining different fabric textures and patterns. Her designs often reflect a fusion of Indian and global fashion influences.

3. Tarun Tahiliani: Tarun Tahiliani is recognized for his luxurious and glamorous saree creations. His designs combine traditional Indian aesthetics with contemporary silhouettes, intricate embellishments, and a play of colors. Tarun Tahiliani has contributed

to the revival of traditional textile techniques and the promotion of Indian craftsmanship on a global scale.

4. Gaurang Shah: Gaurang Shah is renowned for his revival and reinterpretation of traditional handloom sarees. He works closely with skilled artisans and weavers to create handwoven sarees using ancient weaving techniques. Gaurang's designs showcase the beauty of Indian textiles, intricate patterns, and vibrant colors, making him a leading advocate for sustainable fashion and handloom traditions.

5. Masaba Gupta: Masaba Gupta is known for her bold and contemporary take on saree design. Her designs often feature unconventional prints, vibrant colors, and unique draping styles. Masaba's creations appeal to a younger audience and have played a significant role in breaking traditional stereotypes associated with sarees.

6. Raw Mango (Sanjay Garg): Raw Mango is a brand known for its focus on reviving traditional textiles, particularly from the regions of Banaras and Rajasthan. Sanjay Garg, the designer behind Raw Mango, has reimagined traditional sarees with modern color palettes, minimalist motifs, and a clean aesthetic. His designs have garnered international acclaim and contributed to the promotion of handwoven textiles.

These are just a few examples of the many talented contemporary saree designers who have brought fresh perspectives and creative innovations to the saree industry. Their contributions have not only revitalized the popularity of sarees but also played a significant role in preserving traditional craftsmanship and promoting sustainable fashion practices.

Fusion saree trends

Fusion saree trends have gained popularity in recent years as they offer a contemporary twist to the traditional saree, combining elements from different cultures, styles, and fabrics. Here are some notable fusion saree trends:

1. Indo-Western Fusion: This trend combines traditional Indian textiles and draping styles with Western influences. It often involves pairing sarees with Western-inspired blouses, such as crop tops, off-shoulder tops, or shirts. The fusion of Indian and Western aesthetics creates a modern and edgy look.

2. Saree Gowns: Saree gowns offer a fusion of a saree and a gown, creating a seamless blend of the two styles. The upper part resembles a gown or a dress, while the lower part features draped saree pleats. Saree gowns are versatile and easy to wear, making them a popular choice for special occasions.

3. Pant Sarees: Pant sarees combine the elegance of a saree with the comfort and ease of pants. Instead of a traditional petticoat, these sarees are draped over pants or palazzos, giving a contemporary and relaxed look. Pant sarees are perfect for those who prefer a more modern and hassle-free saree experience.

4. Lehenga Sarees: Lehenga sarees merge the beauty of a lehenga and a saree, creating a stunning ensemble. The lower part resembles a lehenga skirt, while the pallu is draped like a saree. Lehenga sarees are popular for weddings and festive occasions, offering a glamorous and regal appearance.

5. Jacketed Sarees: Jacketed sarees feature a saree paired with a matching or contrasting jacket. The jacket adds an extra layer of style and can be designed with various embellishments, embroideries, or modern cuts. Jacketed sarees provide a contemporary and chic look while maintaining the essence of a saree.

6. Saree with Pants: Wearing sarees with pants instead of traditional petticoats has become a popular fusion trend. It offers a comfortable and modern alternative, allowing for more movement and versatility. Sarees with pants can be paired with different types of tops or blouses to create unique and stylish ensembles.

Fusion saree trends allow individuals to experiment with different styles, mix cultural influences, and create their own fashion statements. These trends have brought a fresh and dynamic perspective to the traditional saree, appealing to a wider audience and reflecting the evolving preferences of modern fashion enthusiasts.

Experimental draping styles and innovative saree designs

Experimental draping styles and innovative saree designs have revolutionized the traditional saree, bringing a contemporary and avant-garde touch to this iconic garment. Designers and fashion enthusiasts have pushed the boundaries of saree draping techniques, resulting in stunning and unconventional looks. Here are some examples of experimental draping styles and innovative saree designs:

1. Butterfly Draping: Butterfly draping involves pleating the pallu of the saree to resemble butterfly wings. This unique draping style creates a dramatic and voluminous effect, adding a whimsical touch to the overall look.

2. Mermaid Draping: Inspired by the silhouette of a mermaid's tail, mermaid draping involves tightly pleating the lower portion of the saree, resembling a fishtail. This style accentuates the curves and creates a graceful and ethereal appearance.

3. Cowl Draping: Cowl draping involves creating soft, draped folds in the pallu of the saree, resembling the drapes of a cowl neck. This style adds a contemporary and sophisticated touch to the saree, giving it a high-fashion appeal.

4. Belted Sarees: Adding a belt to the saree has become a popular trend, providing a modern and structured look. The belt cinches the waist and adds definition to the silhouette, while also allowing for ease of movement and ensuring the saree stays in place.

5. Layered Sarees: Layered sarees involve draping multiple layers of fabric to create a dimensional and textured look. Layers can be added in the pallu, skirt, or blouse, resulting in a visually striking and unique saree design.

6. Saree with Cape: The combination of a saree with a cape or capelet adds a contemporary and elegant touch. The cape can be designed in various lengths and styles, offering a stylish alternative to traditional saree blouses.

7. Concept Sarees: Concept sarees are innovative and unconventional designs that challenge the traditional draping styles and silhouettes. These sarees experiment with asymmetrical cuts, unique pleating techniques, and unexpected fabric combinations, resulting in artistic and statement-making ensembles.

8. Saree Gowns: Saree gowns, as mentioned earlier, fuse the elements of a saree and a gown, creating a seamless and modern look. These gowns feature draped pleats, a fitted bodice, and a flowing silhouette, offering a contemporary twist to traditional saree draping.

These experimental draping styles and innovative saree designs showcase the versatility and adaptability of this timeless garment. They push the boundaries of creativity, allowing individuals to express their personal style and make bold fashion statements. With each new design, the saree evolves and transforms, continuing to captivate the fashion world with its endless possibilities.

Global influence and popularity of sarees

The influence and popularity of sarees have transcended borders and gained global recognition. The beauty, elegance, and cultural significance of sarees have attracted people from different parts of the world, leading to its widespread popularity and adoption in various international settings. Here are some ways in which sarees have gained global influence:

1. Red Carpet Appearances: Sarees have graced red carpets and international events, worn by celebrities and fashion icons. Bollywood celebrities, in particular, have played a significant role in showcasing sarees on international platforms, creating a global fascination for this traditional attire.

2. Fashion Shows and Exhibitions: Sarees have become a prominent feature in international fashion shows and exhibitions, where designers from different cultures and backgrounds incorporate elements of saree draping and design into their collections. This exposure helps in introducing sarees to a global audience and promotes cross-cultural fashion appreciation.

3. Cultural Exchanges and Festivals: Cultural exchanges and festivals provide a platform for the display and promotion of traditional garments, including sarees. Through these events, people from diverse backgrounds have the opportunity to witness the beauty and richness of sarees, fostering an appreciation for their craftsmanship and cultural significance.

4. Online Retail and E-commerce: The advent of online retail and e-commerce platforms has made sarees

accessible to a global audience. Customers from different parts of the world can explore and purchase sarees of their choice, contributing to the popularity and reach of this traditional garment beyond geographical boundaries.

5. Fashion Influencers and Social Media: Fashion influencers and social media platforms have played a crucial role in popularizing sarees globally. Influencers from various countries share their unique interpretations of saree styling, creating a global community of saree enthusiasts and inspiring others to embrace this iconic garment.

6. Destination Weddings and Celebrations: Indian weddings and celebrations, including destination weddings, have become popular among individuals from different cultures. Sarees are often chosen as the attire of choice for these events, allowing people to experience and appreciate the beauty of this traditional garment.

7. Collaborations and Fusion Designs: Designers and brands around the world have started collaborating with Indian artisans and weavers to create fusion designs that blend traditional saree elements with contemporary fashion trends. These collaborations not only bring sarees to international markets but also introduce innovative designs that appeal to a wider audience.

The global influence and popularity of sarees signify the universal appeal and timeless charm of this garment. Its versatility, intricate craftsmanship, and connection to cultural heritage continue to captivate individuals worldwide, making sarees a symbol of elegance and grace across borders.

Sarees in the international fashion scene

Sarees have made a significant impact on the international fashion scene, captivating designers, fashion enthusiasts, and celebrities around the world. Here are some notable aspects of sarees' presence in the international fashion scene:

1. Runway Shows: Sarees have graced the runways of prestigious fashion weeks globally, including Paris, New York, London, and Milan. Renowned fashion designers have incorporated sarees into their collections, showcasing their creativity and appreciation for this traditional garment on an international platform.

2. Celebrity Endorsement: Celebrities from various fields, including Hollywood stars, have embraced sarees for red carpet events, award ceremonies, and international film festivals. Their stunning appearances in sarees have garnered attention and appreciation, further highlighting the allure and elegance of this attire.

3. International Collaborations: Indian designers and saree brands have collaborated with international designers, celebrities, and fashion houses to create exclusive collections that fuse traditional Indian craftsmanship with contemporary design aesthetics. These collaborations have helped in promoting sarees on a global scale and introducing them to new audiences.

4. Fashion Publications and Editorials: Leading fashion publications feature sarees in their editorials and fashion spreads, showcasing the versatility and beauty of this traditional garment. These platforms contribute

to the visibility and acceptance of sarees in the international fashion community.

5. Red Carpet Influence: Sarees have become a popular choice for international red carpet events, with celebrities and fashion influencers opting to wear them for their unique and glamorous appeal. The influence of these high-profile appearances helps in elevating the status of sarees as a fashionable and sophisticated choice.

6. Cultural Fusion: Sarees have inspired designers and fashion enthusiasts globally to experiment with fusion styles, combining traditional Indian draping techniques with contemporary silhouettes, fabrics, and patterns. This fusion approach has created a new wave of saree designs that cater to a broader range of preferences and resonate with a global audience.

7. Saree Revival: The interest and demand for sarees among international audiences have led to a resurgence of traditional handloom techniques and craftsmanship. Artisans and weavers from India have gained recognition and opportunities to showcase their skills on international platforms, contributing to the preservation and revival of traditional saree-making techniques.

The presence of sarees in the international fashion scene reflects their timeless appeal, exquisite craftsmanship, and ability to transcend cultural boundaries. They have become an emblem of elegance, sophistication, and cultural exchange, symbolizing the richness of Indian textiles and craftsmanship in the global fashion arena.

Cultural appropriation and appreciation of sarees

The topic of cultural appropriation is an important consideration when discussing the global popularity of sarees and their incorporation into international fashion. It is essential to differentiate between cultural appreciation and cultural appropriation to ensure respectful engagement with diverse cultural traditions. Here are some key points to understand the distinction:

Cultural Appreciation: Cultural appreciation involves recognizing, respecting, and celebrating the cultural significance and beauty of sarees. It involves an authentic interest in understanding the historical, social, and artistic aspects of the garment. Cultural appreciation promotes cross-cultural understanding, fosters dialogue, and honors the cultural heritage associated with sarees. This can be done through collaborations, learning from artisans and weavers, promoting ethical sourcing, and showcasing diverse voices within the industry.

Cultural Appropriation: Cultural appropriation, on the other hand, refers to the adoption or borrowing of elements from another culture without proper understanding, respect, or permission. It often involves commodifying cultural symbols or practices without acknowledging their historical or social context. This can be harmful and offensive, especially when done for profit or to reinforce stereotypes. It is important to avoid appropriating sacred symbols, misrepresenting cultural traditions, or engaging in cultural caricatures when incorporating elements of the saree into fashion or popular culture.

Promoting Cultural Exchange: The key lies in promoting cultural exchange that is respectful, inclusive, and mutually beneficial. This involves acknowledging and giving credit to the cultural origins of sarees, collaborating with artisans and weavers, supporting ethical and sustainable practices, and fostering dialogue between cultures. By engaging in cultural exchange with sensitivity and understanding, the global fashion community can appreciate and draw inspiration from the beauty of sarees while respecting their cultural significance.

Education and Awareness: Education plays a crucial role in fostering cultural appreciation and understanding. It is important for designers, consumers, and the general public to educate themselves about the history, significance, and cultural context of sarees. This knowledge helps to avoid stereotypes, misconceptions, and inadvertent cultural appropriation. By embracing a learning mindset and engaging in respectful dialogue, individuals can develop a deeper appreciation for sarees and contribute to a more inclusive and respectful fashion landscape.

By navigating the fine line between cultural appreciation and appropriation, individuals and industries can celebrate the beauty and significance of sarees while ensuring that their adoption and promotion are done in a respectful and responsible manner.

Celebrating the timeless beauty and cultural heritage of sarees

Sarees, with their rich history, intricate craftsmanship, and timeless elegance, are more than just garments. They are a celebration of the cultural heritage and artistic traditions that have been passed down through generations. Each saree tells a story, weaving together threads of craftsmanship, regional diversity, and personal narratives.

The beauty of sarees lies not only in their exquisite designs but also in the cultural significance they carry. They symbolize tradition, grace, and femininity, reflecting the unique identity of different communities and regions. From the vibrant colors and intricate weaves of Banarasi sarees to the resplendent silk of Kanchivaram sarees, each style has its own distinct charm.

Sarees are not confined to a particular era or trend; they transcend time, effortlessly blending tradition with contemporary styles. They have evolved over the years, adapting to changing fashion sensibilities while preserving their essence. Today, sarees are embraced by women around the world, not only as a symbol of cultural heritage but also as a statement of personal style.

The craftsmanship involved in creating sarees is awe-inspiring. Skilled artisans and weavers invest hours of meticulous work into every saree, from selecting the finest fabrics to hand-weaving intricate patterns and motifs. Their dedication and expertise are vital in preserving the artistry and ensuring the quality of sarees.

The popularity of sarees extends beyond cultural boundaries.

They have captured the attention of the global fashion industry, gracing runways, red carpets, and international events. Designers, both in India and abroad, have been inspired by the versatility and elegance of sarees, incorporating elements of this iconic garment into their collections. This fusion of traditional and contemporary aesthetics has given rise to innovative designs and reinvented draping styles.

In celebrating the timeless beauty and cultural heritage of sarees, we honor the skills of the artisans, weavers, and designers who contribute to their creation. We embrace the diversity of styles and techniques, appreciating the stories they tell and the emotions they evoke. By wearing sarees, we become ambassadors of cultural heritage, promoting its preservation and spreading its allure to the world.

Whether worn on special occasions, festive celebrations, or in daily life, sarees continue to inspire and captivate. They are a testament to the enduring legacy of craftsmanship, the beauty of cultural diversity, and the power of fashion to transcend borders. By cherishing and celebrating sarees, we pay homage to the timeless traditions and exquisite artistry that make them an irreplaceable part of our cultural heritage.

Sarees as a symbol of empowerment and identity

Sarees are not just pieces of fabric; they hold immense symbolic value as a symbol of empowerment and identity for women. Through their elegant drape and intricate designs, sarees empower women to embrace their femininity, grace, and individuality.

Sarees have been worn by women across different cultures and regions for centuries, representing their strength, resilience, and cultural heritage. They serve as a powerful expression of identity, reflecting the unique traditions, customs, and values of a community or region. By wearing a saree, women not only connect with their roots but also assert their individuality and proudly showcase their heritage.

The act of wearing a saree involves a sense of agency and self-expression. It allows women to choose from a wide variety of fabrics, colors, patterns, and styles, enabling them to curate their own personal narrative. From the vibrant hues of a Bandhani saree to the understated elegance of a Tussar silk saree, each choice reflects a woman's taste, personality, and sense of style.

Sarees also provide a platform for women to express their creativity and support artisanal traditions. The handloom industry, which produces exquisite sarees, empowers local artisans and weavers, especially women, by providing them with livelihood opportunities and preserving their traditional skills. By supporting handloom sarees, women contribute to the sustainability of the craft and empower communities.

Furthermore, sarees are often worn during significant milestones and celebrations in a woman's life, such as weddings, festivals, and special occasions. They become a symbol of pride and accomplishment, embodying the journey, achievements, and dreams of a woman. Sarees hold sentimental value, passed down through generations as family heirlooms, carrying with them stories of love, heritage, and strength.

In a world where women continue to strive for equality and empowerment, sarees serve as a reminder of the inherent strength and resilience of women. They celebrate femininity, self-expression, and the diverse identities of women. Sarees transcend societal norms and expectations, allowing women to embrace their bodies, express their personal style, and stand tall with confidence.

By wearing a saree, a woman becomes part of a legacy of strong and empowered women who have adorned this timeless garment for centuries. It is a statement of empowerment, asserting her place in the world while honoring her cultural heritage. Sarees are not just garments; they are a powerful symbol of empowerment, identity, and the beauty of being a woman.

Embracing the versatility and elegance of sarees in modern times

In today's modern world, sarees continue to captivate and inspire women with their versatility and timeless elegance. While sarees hold deep cultural and traditional roots, they have also evolved to adapt to the changing tastes and preferences of contemporary fashion.

One of the reasons sarees remain relevant and cherished is their ability to effortlessly blend tradition with modernity. Designers and fashion enthusiasts have pushed the boundaries of saree draping, infusing it with innovative styles and experimental designs. From contemporary draping techniques to unconventional fabric choices, sarees have embraced a fresh and dynamic outlook, appealing to women of all ages.

The versatility of sarees allows women to explore a myriad of looks and styles. They can be adorned with intricate embroideries, sequins, and embellishments for a glamorous and festive look, or with minimalist designs and clean lines for a sophisticated and understated appearance. The wide range of fabrics, from lightweight georgette to luxurious silk, offers endless possibilities to suit various occasions and personal preferences.

Sarees have also become a canvas for artistic expression and creativity. Designers and artisans are constantly reinventing traditional motifs and patterns, incorporating contemporary elements and global influences. This fusion of traditional craftsmanship with modern aesthetics has given rise to unique and eclectic saree designs that resonate with the tastes of the modern woman.

The adaptability of sarees extends beyond formal occasions and special events. Casual and daily wear sarees have gained popularity, offering comfort and style for everyday wear. Lightweight fabrics, minimalistic designs, and easy-to-drape options have made sarees accessible and practical for women in their day-to-day lives.

Moreover, sarees have transcended geographical boundaries and gained recognition on the global fashion stage. International fashion runways and red carpets have witnessed the grace and allure of sarees, with celebrities and fashion influencers embracing them as a symbol of elegance and sophistication. The increasing demand for sarees from global markets has led to collaborations between designers from different countries, resulting in fusion creations that celebrate diverse cultures.

In embracing the versatility and elegance of sarees, women not only celebrate their own beauty but also contribute to the preservation of traditional craftsmanship and support the livelihoods of artisans and weavers. By choosing sarees as part of their wardrobe, women become ambassadors of culture and style, bridging the gap between tradition and modernity.

In the fast-paced world of fashion, sarees have stood the test of time, evolving and adapting to contemporary sensibilities. They continue to inspire women to embrace their individuality, celebrate their heritage, and radiate confidence and grace. Sarees are more than just garments; they are a reflection of a woman's personality, a celebration of her uniqueness, and a timeless symbol of elegance in the modern era.